Table of Contents

(Answer Key in Back)

Name: _____

Score:

Front

Back

What is it called?

① _____   ② _____   ③ _____

What is its value?

④ _____ ¢   ⑤ _____ ¢   ⑥ _____ ¢

Write the value of each group of coins.

⑦ _____ ¢

⑧ _____ ¢

⑨ _____ ¢

⑩ _____ ¢

Add the following values. (Don't forget to include the money symbol after your answer.)

⑪
  12¢
+ 8¢

⑫
  26¢
+10¢

⑬
   5¢
+53¢

⑭
  32¢
+19¢

⑮
  16¢
+76¢

⑯
  22¢
+37¢

⑰
   4¢
+11¢

⑱
  38¢
+45¢

⑲
  62¢
+ 9¢

⑳
  80¢
+10¢

Day 2

Dimes, Nickels, Pennies

Name: _____

Score:

Write the value of each group of coins.

① _____ ¢

② _____ ¢

③ _____ ¢

④ _____ ¢

Write the value of each group of coins.

⑤ 2 Dimes
1 Nickel
3 Pennies   _____ ¢

⑥ 1 Dime
2 Nickels
6 Pennies   _____ ¢

⑦ 2 Dimes
6 Nickels   _____ ¢

⑧ 2 Dimes
2 Nickels
8 Pennies   _____ ¢

⑨ 1 Nickel
12 Pennies   _____ ¢

⑩ 4 Dimes
4 Nickels
7 Pennies   _____ ¢

⑪ 5 Dimes
1 Nickel
4 Pennies   _____ ¢

⑫ 2 Dimes
1 Nickel
16 Pennies   _____ ¢

Day 3

Dimes, Nickels, Pennies

Name: _____

Score:

Shade the option that has an equivalent value?

①

- Ⓐ 5 nickels, 7 pennies
- Ⓑ 1 dime, 3 nickels, 2 pennies
- Ⓒ 2 dimes, 1 nickel, 2 pennies
- Ⓓ 1 dime, 2 nickels, 7 pennies

②

- Ⓐ 3 nickels, 2 pennies
- Ⓑ 2 nickels, 2 pennies
- Ⓒ 1 dime, 2 pennies
- Ⓓ 1 dime, 2 nickels, 2 pennies

③

- Ⓐ 1 dime, 15 pennies
- Ⓑ 3 nickels, 6 pennies
- Ⓒ 2 dimes, 6 pennies
- Ⓓ 2 dimes, 2 pennies

④

- Ⓐ 2 dimes, 6 nickels
- Ⓑ 3 dimes
- Ⓒ 4 nickels
- Ⓓ 3 dimes, 2 nickels, 5 pennies

⑤

- Ⓐ 4 dimes, 1 nickel
- Ⓑ 1 dime, 4 nickels
- Ⓒ 3 dimes, 1 penny
- Ⓓ 1 dime, 5 nickels

⑥

- Ⓐ 13 pennies
- Ⓑ 3 nickels, 3 pennies
- Ⓒ 3 nickels, 8 pennies
- Ⓓ 6 nickels, 3 pennies

⑦

- Ⓐ 1 dime, 3 nickels, 7 pennies
- Ⓑ 1 quarter, 7 pennies
- Ⓒ 18 pennies
- Ⓓ 1 quarter, 2 pennies

⑧

- Ⓐ 3 nickels 6 pennies
- Ⓑ 1 dime, 3 nickels,
- Ⓒ 1 dime, 6 pennies
- Ⓓ 3 dimes, 1 penny

Day 4
Quarters

Name: _____

Score:

Counting Quarters   <u>What is its value?</u>

 ① _____25___ ¢

②  _____ ¢

③  _____ ¢

④  _____ ¢

Write the value for each group of coins.

⑤ _____ ¢   ⑥ _____ ¢

⑦ _____ ¢   ⑧ _____ ¢

⑨ _____ ¢   ⑩ _____ ¢

Day 5

Counting Less than $1

Name: _____

Score:

Write the value for each group of coins.

① _____ ₵

② _____ ₵

③ _____ ₵

④ _____ ₵

⑤ _____ ₵

⑥ _____ ₵

⑦ _____ ₵

⑧ _____ ₵

Day 6
Counting Less than $1

Write the value for each group of coins.

① _____ ¢

② _____ ¢

③ _____ ¢

④ _____ ¢

Write the value of each group of coins.

⑤ 2 Quarters
2 Dimes
1 Nickel   _____ ¢
1 Pennies

⑥ 3 Quarters
3 Nickels   _____ ¢
8 Pennies

⑦ 1 Quarter
3 Dimes
2 Nickels   _____ ¢
17 Pennies

⑧ 2 Quarters
5 Nickels   _____ ¢

⑨ 3 Quarters
1 Dime   _____ ¢
2 Pennies

⑩ 1 Quarter
2 Dimes   _____ ¢
21 Pennies

⑪ 2 Quarters
1 Dime
3 Nickels   _____ ¢
4 Pennies

⑫ 3 Quarters
1 Dime   _____ ¢
1 Nickel

Name: _____

Solve the following word problems.

① Ben has 34¢ and Sonia has 50¢. How much money do they have together?

② Angela bought a pencil for 35¢ and a notebook for 49¢. How much did she spend?

③ Jason had a quarter and 3 nickels, then he found 4 dimes. How much money does Jason have now?

④ Rebecca was given a dime and a nickel for taking out the trash and two quarters for weeding the garden. How much money did she earn?

⑤ Tyler had 6 nickels and 8 pennies, then his grandmother gave him a quarter for his birthday. How much money does Tyler have now?

⑥ Rachel wants to buy a bracelet for herself and a bracelet for her friend. Each bracelet costs 39¢. How much money will Rachel need?

⑦ Grace has 72¢. Her little brother has 16¢. How much do they have together?

⑧ Ava has a lemonade stand. She earned a quarter and 7 pennies in the morning. In the afternoon she earned 3 dimes and 3 nickels. How much money did she make all together?

Day 8
Word Problems

Name: _____

Score:

Subtract the following values. (Don't forget to include the money symbol.)

①
```
  76¢
- 54¢
```

②
```
  31¢
- 10¢
```

③
```
  42¢
- 13¢
```

④
```
  95¢
- 29¢
```

⑤
```
  58¢
- 55¢
```

⑥
```
  81¢
-  7¢
```

⑦
```
  60¢
- 45¢
```

⑧
```
  22¢
- 12¢
```

⑨
```
  38¢
-  6¢
```

⑩
```
  75¢
- 28¢
```

Solve the following word problems.

⑪ Evan had 3 quarters and 2 dimes, then he bought a toy car for 59¢. How much money did he have left after the purchase?

⑫ Luke has 72¢. His sister has 2 quarters and a nickel. How much more money does Luke have than his sister?

⑬ Ruby had 4 dimes and 4 nickels, then she bought a pack of gum for 35¢. How much money did Ruby have after the purchase?

⑭ Darcie had 50¢, until she lost a dime and 8 pennies when they fell from a hole in her pocket. How much money does she have left?

⑮ Mike wants to buy a hotdog. It costs 99¢. He only has a quarter and 2 pennies in his pocket. How much more money does he need to buy the hotdog?

© Libro Studio LLC 2020

Name: _____

Score:

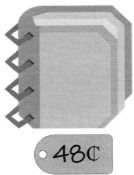   

48¢   19¢   12¢   5¢

Use the images above to solve each problem.

① Holly has 16¢. How much more money would she need to buy an apple?

② William wants to buy 2 notebooks. How much money will that cost?

③ Lola gives the clerk 3 quarters when buying a notebook and an apple. How much change should the clerk give Lola back?

④ Rebecca has a quarter, a dime, and 7 pennies. How many crayons can she buy?

⑤ Archie has 2 quarters and 7 nickels. How much money would he have left if he buys a spiral notebook and an apple?

⑥ Logan had a quarter, 4 dimes, 3 nickels, and 13 pennies before buying 2 pencils. How much money does he have now?

Name: _____

Score:

Counting Quarters

What is its value?

① $ _0.25_

② $ _____

③ $ _____

④ $ _____

⑤ $ _____

⑥ $ _____

⑦ $ _____

⑧ $ _____

Write the value of each group of coins.

⑨ 12 quarters $ _____

⑩ 10 quarters $ _____

⑪ 23 quarters $ _____

⑫ 29 quarters $ _____

Day 11

Name: _____

Score:

Add the following values. (Don't forget to include the dollar symbol.)

① $1.22 +$0.65 ② $1.04 +$3.18 ③ $7.92 +$0.99 ④ $5.81 +$6.59 ⑤ $0.70 +$8.25

Write the value of each group of coins.

⑥ $_____

⑦ $_____

⑧ $_____

⑨ $_____

Write the value of each group of coins.

⑩ 6 Quarters
5 Dimes
14 Pennies $_____

⑪ 11 Quarters
1 Dime
4 Nickels $_____

⑫ 15 Quarters
4 Dimes
5 Pennies $_____

⑬ 8 Quarters
3 Dimes
2 Nickels
9 Pennies $_____

⑭ 12 Quarters
1 Dime
1 Nickel
24 Pennies $_____

⑮ 10 Quarters
8 Dimes
2 Nickels
7 Pennies $_____

Day 12

Exchanging Coins

Make each problem equivalent.

① 5 🪙 = ___ 🪙

② 4 🪙 = ___ 🪙

③ 1 🪙 = ___ 🪙

④ 2 🪙 = ___ 🪙

⑤ 5 🪙 = ___ 🪙

⑥ 2 🪙 = ___ 🪙

⑦ 6 🪙 = ___ 🪙

⑧ 5 🪙 = ___ 🪙

⑨ 75 🪙 = ___ 🪙

⑩ 2 🪙 = ___ 🪙

⑪ 7 🪙 = ___ 🪙

⑫ 16 🪙 = ___ 🪙

⑬ 2 🪙 = ___ 🪙

⑭ 4 🪙 = ___ 🪙

⑮ 90 🪙 = ___ 🪙

⑯ 3 🪙 = ___ 🪙

Name: _____

Subtract the following values. (Don't forget to include the dollar symbol.)

① $6.89
−$3.50

② $8.29
−$0.75

③ $5.98
−$5.27

④ $9.70
−$1.64

⑤ $0.81
−$0.25

Solve the following word problems.

⑥ Phoebe had $4.25, then she earned $2.75 for babysitting. How much money does she have now?

⑦ Theo has $2.44 and Clair has $5.27. How much is that together?

⑧ The library charges a quarter each day a book is late. Ivy had one book that was 5 days late. If she had $5.81 before paying this fee, how much does she have after the fee is paid?

⑨ Henry has $2.73. He wants to buy a video game that costs $8.00. How much more money does he need?

⑩ Dylan picked fruit for two days. The farmer paid him $3.50 the first day and $4.25 the second day. How much did he earn all together?

⑪ Lexi had $7.82, then she bought a stuffed animal for $5.99. How much money does she have after the purchase?

⑫ Hannah has $6.40 and Edward has $8.21. How much more money does Edward have than Hannah?

Name: _____

Score:

Hamburger	Taco	Pie	Doughnut	Ice-Cream	Cookie

 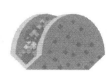

$4.97	$4.35	$3.50	$2.29	$1.15	$0.89

Use the images above to solve each problem.

① Hugo wants to buy a hamburger and a cookie. How much money will he need?

② Mia has 11 quarters 4 nickels and 9 pennies. How much more money does she need to buy a slice of pie?

③ Jaxon orders a hamburger. His brother orders a taco. How much do their meals cost all together?

④ Esme wants to order a doughnut for herself and one for each of her two friends. How much money will she need?

⑤ Albert hands 6 quarters to the clerk and asks for an ice-cream cone. The clerk gives Albert one coin for his change. What coin is it?
(Hint: How much change should Albert receive?)

⑥ Isabelle has $8.72. She buys a taco and a doughnut. How much money does she have left?

Day 15
Counting Small Bills

Name: _____

Score:

Front			
Back			

What is it called?	① _____	② _____	③ _____
What is its value?	④ $_____	⑤ $_____	⑥ $_____

Write the value of each group of bills.

⑦ $_____

⑧ $_____

⑨ $_____

⑩ $_____

Name: _____

Score:

Write the value of each group.

① $_____

② $_____

③ $_____

④ $_____

Write the value of each group.

⑤ 6 Tens
2 Fives
7 Ones $_____

⑥ 4 Tens
4 Fives
2 Ones $_____

⑦ 3 Tens
1 Five
8 Ones $_____

⑧ 7 Fives
16 Ones $_____

⑨ 5 Tens
5 Fives
5 Ones $_____

⑩ 2 Tens
11 Fives
24 Ones $_____

Name: _____

Score:

Make each problem equivalent.

① 4 = _____

② 1  = _____

③ 12 = _____

④ 1  = _____

⑤ 1  = _____

⑥ 3  = _____

⑦ 1  = _____

⑧ 1  = _____

⑨ 10  = _____

⑩ 40  = _____

Name: _____

Score:

Write the value of each group.

① $ _____

② $ _____

③ $ _____

④ $ _____

⑤ $ _____

⑥ $ _____

⑦ $ _____

⑧ $ _____

Day 19

Word Problems

Name: _____

Score:

Subtract the following values. (Don't forget to include the dollar symbol.)

① $62.48
−$8.93

② $15.75
−$4.16

③ $53.39
−$15.27

④ $47.13
−$17.63

⑤ $90.42
−$36.77

Solve the following word problems.

⑥ Teddy was given 35 dollars for his birthday. He bought a new baseball bat for $18.55. How much money does he have left?

⑦ Emily has $46.20. She wants to buy a new e-reader tablet. It costs $80.99. How much more money does she need to save?

⑧ Arlo has a fifty-dollar bill and a twenty-dollar bill. Ken has $41.37. How much more money does Arlo have than Ken?

⑨ Freya has $8.26 and Clair has $26.07. How much money do they have together?

⑩ Henry wants to buy a shirt for $16.99 and some socks for $5.75. How much money will these items cost?

⑪ Evelyn had $14.71. She then received 2 ten-dollar bills and a five-dollar bill for her birthday. How much money does she have now?

⑫ Elliot earns fifteen dollars every time he mows the lawn. He mows the lawn three times. How much more does he need to save to buy a skateboard that costs $72.45?

Name: _____

Bike — $89.99
Scooter — $45.00
Basketball — $17.85
Baseball — $7.00

Use the images above to solve each problem.

① Daisy Is saving her money for a scooter. If she has $17.64 now, how much more money will she need to save?

② David wants to buy a basketball and a baseball. How much money will he need?

③ Mr. Kelly wants to buy 4 baseballs for his gym class. How much money will he need?

④ Reuben wants to buy a bike. He currently has 3 twenty-dollar bills and 12 one-dollar bills. How much more money does he need?

⑤ Leo and his sister both want a scooter. How much money will they need to buy them?

⑥ How much more does a scooter cost than a basketball?

Name: _____

Score:

	Front		
Front			
Back			
What is it called?	① _____	② _____	③ _____
What is its value?	④ $_____	⑤ $_____	⑥ $_____

Write the value of each group of bills.

⑦ $_____

⑧ $_____

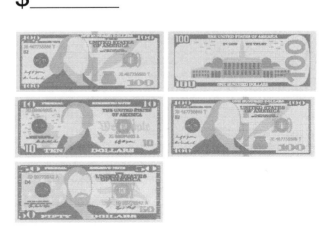

⑨ $_____

⑩ $_____

Day 22

Counting Bills and Coins

Name: _____

Score:

Write the value of each group.

① $ _____

② $ _____

③ $ _____

④ $ _____

Write the value of each group.

⑤ 6 Tens
2 Fives
7 Ones $ _____
3 Quarters
2 Dimes

⑥ 2 Hundreds
4 Tens
1 Five $ _____
2 Ones
4 Quarters
1 Nickel

⑦ 1 Fifty
4 Twenties
3 Tens $ _____
2 Ones
9 Quarters
5 Dimes
2 Pennies

⑧ 3 Hundreds
3 Twenties
4 Fives $ _____
16 Ones
7 Dimes
8 Nickels

Day 23

Exchanging Bills

Name: _____

Score:

Find the equivalet value for each problem.

① 1  = ____

② 2  = ____

③ 1  = ____

④ 1  = ____

⑤ 1  = ____

Write the value for each group.

⑥ $_____

⑦ $_____

⑧ $_____

⑨ $_____

© Libro Studio LLC 2020

Name: _____

Subtract the following values. (Don't forget to include the dollar symbol.)

① $132.08
−$47.10

② $401.29
−$171.34

③ $685.98
−$609.51

④ $200.00
−$21.75

Solve the following word problems.

⑤ Sara is looking at computers. The first computer costs $349.50. The second costs $275.00. How much more is the first computer?

⑥ Sara wants the computer that costs $275.00. She currently has $190.45 saved. How much more money does she need to buy it?

⑦ Oscar was paid $250.00 for painting a house and $160.00 for painting the garage. How much money did he make?

⑧ Jack has $329.61 and Jerry has $570.15. How much more money does Jerry have than Jack?

⑨ Laura has 4 hundreds, 3 fifties, and 6 twenty-dollar bills. How much money does she have?

⑩ Maria had $146.50 before buying concert tickets. If the tickets were $65.99, how much money does she have after the purchase?

⑪ Isaac and Josh want to buy an $800.00 fishing boat together. Isaac has $351.00 saved. Josh has $368.25 saved. How much more money do they need before they can buy the boat?

Day 25
Word Problems

Name: _____

Score:

Ring — $950.99
Telescope — $675.00
Motorized Scooter — $479.00
Violin — $320.00
Game Controller — $49.99

Use the images above to solve each problem.

① Joshua wants to buy 4 video game controllers. How much money will he need for this purchase?

② Maryam wants to by a telescope. She currently has $426.00 saved. How much more money does she need to save?

③ Bella uses 5 hundred-dollar bills to buy a motorized scooter. How much money should she receive in change?

④ Lucas wants to buy a diamond ring. He currently has 770.00 saved. How much more money does he need to buy the ring?

⑤ Max needs a new violin. He gives the clerk 2 hundred-dollar bills and 3 fifty-dollar bills. How much should he receive in change?

⑥ Amber also wants to buy a violin. She only has twenty-dollar bills. How many twenties will she need to buy the violin?

Day 26
Making Change

Name: _____

Score:

*Show how to make each value using the **fewest amount of coins**.*

① 19 cents:

___1___ ___1___ ___4___ _____

② 38 cents:

_____ _____ _____ _____

③ 61 cents:

_____ _____ _____ _____

④ 97 cents:

_____ _____ _____ _____

⑤ 83 cents:

_____ _____ _____ _____

⑥ 56 cents:

_____ _____ _____ _____

⑦ 24 cents:

_____ _____ _____ _____

⑧ 45 cents:

_____ _____ _____ _____

⑨ 72 cents:

_____ _____ _____ _____

⑩ 33 cents:

_____ _____ _____ _____

⑪ 26 cents:

_____ _____ _____ _____

⑫ 90 cents:

_____ _____ _____ _____

© Libro Studio LLC 2020

Day 27

Making Change

Name: _____

*Show how to make each value using the **fewest amount of bills and coins.***

① $22.53

 ___

___   ___   ___   ___

② $63.17

 ___

___   ___   ___   ___

③ $48.92

 ___

___   ___   ___   ___

④ $39.70

 ___

___   ___   ___   ___

⑤ $50.49

 ___

___   ___   ___   ___

⑥ $76.88

 ___

___   ___   ___   ___

Name: _____

Score:

*Show how to make each value using the **fewest amount of bills and coins**.*

① $14.72

 ____

 ____

____

② $7.55

 ____

 ____

____

③ $18.43

 ____

 ____

____

④ $79.65

 ____

 ____

____

⑤ $99.99

 ____

 ____

____

⑥ $148.37

 ____

 ____

____

Day 29

Identifying Fractions

Complete the fraction to represent each image.

① 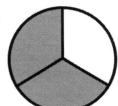 $\dfrac{2}{}$

② 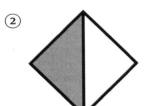 $\dfrac{}{2}$

③ 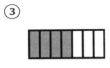 $\dfrac{}{7}$

④  $\dfrac{}{4}$

⑤ 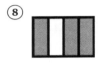 $\dfrac{4}{}$

⑥ 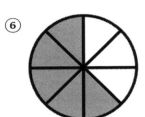 $\dfrac{}{8}$

⑦ 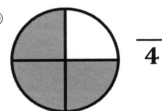 $\dfrac{3}{}$

⑧ 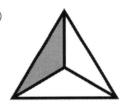 $\dfrac{3}{}$

⑨  $\dfrac{}{12}$

⑩  $\dfrac{}{4}$

⑪ 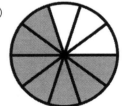 $\dfrac{1}{}$

⑫ 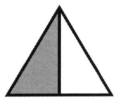 $\dfrac{}{3}$

⑬ 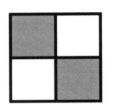 $\dfrac{}{6}$

⑭ 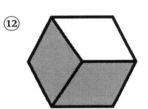 $\dfrac{7}{}$

⑮  $\dfrac{1}{}$

⑯ $\dfrac{}{3}$

⑰  $\dfrac{3}{}$

⑱ 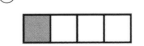 $\dfrac{}{4}$

Day 30
Identifying Fractions

Name: _____

Score:

Write the fraction that represents each image.

①  ____

② 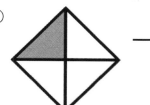 ____

③  ____

④ 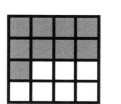 ____

⑤ 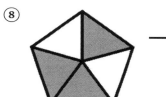 ____

⑥  ____

⑦ 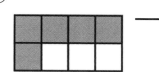 ____

⑧ 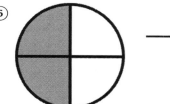 ____

⑨  ____

⑩ 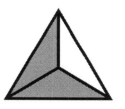 ____

⑪ 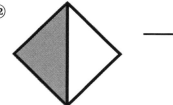 ____

⑫ 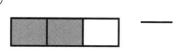 ____

⑬ 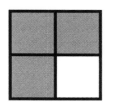 ____

⑭  ____

⑮  ____

⑯  ____

⑰ 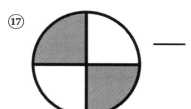 ____

⑱  ____

Day 31
Identifying Fractions

Name: _____

Score:

Problems 1-6: *Answer each question by writing your answer in fraction form.*

①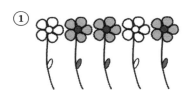

How many of the flowers are dark? _____

②

How many cupcakes have sprinkles? _____

③

How many fish
are swimming down? _____

④

How many ice-creams
are chocolate flavored? _____

⑤

How many candies have stripes? _____

⑥

How many of the shells are white? _____

Problems 7-10: *Write your answer in the blank space provided to make each equation true.*

⑦

$\frac{1}{3}$ of 3 is _____.

⑧

$\frac{3}{4}$ of 4 is _____.

⑨

$\frac{1}{2}$ of 12 is _____.

⑩

$\frac{2}{5}$ of 15 is _____.

© Libro Studio LLC 2020

Day 32
Identifying Fractions

Name: _____

Score:

Problems 1-9: *Write the fraction that represents each image.*

① ___

② 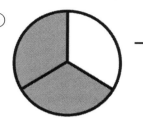 ___

③ 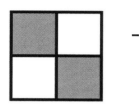 ___

④ 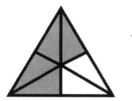 ___

⑤  ___

⑥  ___

⑦  ___

⑧  ___

⑨  ___

Problems 10-18: *Shade each shape to represents the fraction to the right.*

⑩ 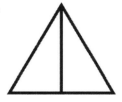 $\dfrac{2}{8}$

⑪  $\dfrac{1}{3}$

⑫  $\dfrac{6}{7}$

⑬  $\dfrac{1}{2}$

⑭  $\dfrac{1}{5}$

⑮ 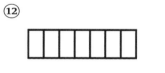 $\dfrac{5}{10}$

⑯  $\dfrac{4}{5}$

⑰  $\dfrac{2}{3}$

⑱ 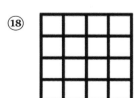 $\dfrac{11}{16}$

Name: _____

Score:

Problems 1-7: *Answer each question by writing your answer in fraction form.*

① *Draw circles around the dots to divide them into 2 equal groups.*

What is $\frac{1}{2}$ of 10? _____

② *Draw circles around the dots to divide them into 5 equal groups.*

What is $\frac{3}{5}$ of 15? _____

③ *Draw circles around the dots to divide them into 4 equal groups.*

What is $\frac{1}{4}$ of 20? _____

④ *Draw circles around the dots to divide them into 3 equal groups.*

What is $\frac{2}{3}$ of 12? _____

⑤ *Draw circles around the dots to divide them into 4 equal groups.*

What is $\frac{3}{4}$ of 8? _____

⑥ *Draw circles around the dots to divide them into 2 equal groups.*

What is $\frac{1}{2}$ of 16? _____

⑦ *Draw circles around the dots to divide them into 6 equal groups.*

What is $\frac{5}{6}$ of 18? _____

Day 34
Identifying Fractions

Name: _____

Score:

Problems 1-4: *Answer each question by writing your answer in fraction form.*

①

How many faces are happy? _____

②

How many faces are wearing a hat? _____

③

How many bikers have
one tire off the ground? _____

④

How many delivery trucks are there? _____

Problems 5-13: *Shade each shape to represents the fraction to the right.*

⑤ 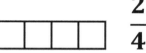 $\dfrac{2}{4}$

⑥ $\dfrac{1}{2}$

⑦ $\dfrac{1}{5}$

⑧ $\dfrac{6}{8}$

⑨  $\dfrac{3}{12}$

⑩ $\dfrac{2}{3}$

⑪  $\dfrac{5}{6}$

⑫ 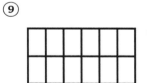 $\dfrac{1}{4}$

⑬  $\dfrac{9}{10}$

Name: _____

Score:

Write the fraction that represents each image.

①  ___

② 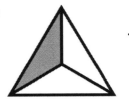 ___

③ 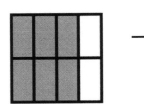 ___

④ 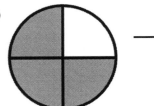 ___

⑤  ___

⑥ 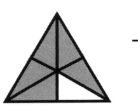 ___

⑦ 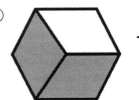 ___

⑧ 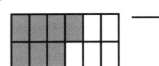 ___

⑨ 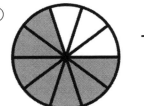 ___

Problems 10-13: *Write your answer in the blank space provided to make each equation true.*

⑩

$\frac{2}{5}$ of 5 is _____.

⑪

$\frac{3}{4}$ of 8 is _____.

⑫

$\frac{1}{2}$ of 6 is _____.

⑬

$\frac{1}{4}$ of 16 is _____.

Name: _____

Score:

Problems 1-6: *Answer each question by writing your answer in fraction form.*

① *Draw circles around the dots to divide them into 3 equal groups.*

What is $\frac{2}{3}$ of 9? ____

② *Draw circles around the dots to divide them into 4 equal groups.*

What is $\frac{1}{4}$ of 24? ____

③ *Draw circles around the dots to divide them into 5 equal groups.*

What is $\frac{3}{5}$ of 25? ____

④ *Draw circles around the dots to divide them into 8 equal groups.*

What is $\frac{7}{8}$ of 16? ____

⑤ *Draw circles around the dots to divide them into 4 equal groups.*

What is $\frac{3}{4}$ of 12? ____

⑥ *Draw circles around the dots to divide them into 2 equal groups.*

What is $\frac{5}{6}$ of 24? ____

⑦ *Draw circles around the dots to divide them into 3 equal groups.*

What is $\frac{1}{3}$ of 6? ____

Day 37

> < =

Name: _____

Score:

Problems 1-6: *Is the fraction on the right greater than (>), less than (<), or equal to (=) the fraction on the left? Look at each shape to help you decide.*

① $\dfrac{1}{3}$ ___ $\dfrac{2}{3}$ (>, < or =)

② $\dfrac{4}{5}$ ___ $\dfrac{4}{5}$ (>, < or =)

③ $\dfrac{6}{8}$ ___ $\dfrac{4}{8}$ (>, < or =)

④ $\dfrac{3}{6}$ ___ $\dfrac{2}{6}$ (>, < or =)

⑤ $\dfrac{2}{4}$ ___ $\dfrac{3}{4}$ (>, < or =)

⑥ $\dfrac{6}{10}$ ___ $\dfrac{4}{10}$ (>, < or =)

⑦ $\dfrac{1}{3}$ ___ $\dfrac{1}{3}$ (>, < or =)

⑧ $\dfrac{4}{12}$ ___ $\dfrac{7}{12}$ (>, < or =)

⑨ $\dfrac{2}{4}$ ___ $\dfrac{2}{4}$ (>, < or =)

⑩ $\dfrac{4}{6}$ ___ $\dfrac{3}{6}$ (>, < or =)

⑪ $\dfrac{2}{8}$ ___ $\dfrac{5}{8}$ (>, < or =)

⑫ 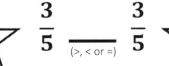 $\dfrac{3}{5}$ ___ $\dfrac{3}{5}$ (>, < or =)

© Libro Studio LLC 2020

Name: _____

Score:

Problems 1-6: *Write your answer in the blank space provided to make each equation true.*

① $\dfrac{1}{2} = \dfrac{}{4}$

② $\dfrac{}{4} = \dfrac{6}{8}$

③ $\dfrac{5}{10} = \dfrac{}{2}$

④ $\dfrac{4}{6} = \dfrac{}{3}$

⑤ $\dfrac{}{6} = \dfrac{2}{4}$

⑥ $\dfrac{2}{8} = \dfrac{}{4}$

Problems 7-14: *Shade the shapes below to determine the equivalent fraction. Write your answer in the blank space provided to make each equation true.*

⑦ $\dfrac{3}{4} = \dfrac{}{8}$

⑧ $\dfrac{3}{6} = \dfrac{}{2}$

⑨ $\dfrac{}{6} = \dfrac{2}{3}$

⑩ $\dfrac{6}{10} = \dfrac{}{5}$

⑪ $\dfrac{1}{3} = \dfrac{}{9}$

⑫ $\dfrac{}{6} = \dfrac{2}{4}$

⑬ $\dfrac{}{10} = \dfrac{4}{5}$

⑭ $\dfrac{1}{4} = \dfrac{}{8}$

Name: _____

Score:

Problems 1-6: *Is the fraction on the right greater than (>), less than (<), or equal to (=) the fraction on the left? Look at each shape to help you decide.*

① $\dfrac{2}{4}$ ___(>, < or =)___ $\dfrac{2}{4}$

② $\dfrac{4}{6}$ ___(>, < or =)___ $\dfrac{3}{6}$

③ $\dfrac{2}{5}$ ___(>, < or =)___ $\dfrac{4}{5}$

④ $\dfrac{5}{8}$ ___(>, < or =)___ $\dfrac{6}{8}$

⑤ $\dfrac{2}{4}$ ___(>, < or =)___ $\dfrac{1}{4}$

⑥ $\dfrac{2}{6}$ ___(>, < or =)___ $\dfrac{2}{6}$

Problems 7-14: *Decided if the fraction on the right is greater than (>), less than (<), or equal to (=) the fraction on the left. Shade the shapes to help you make your decision.*

⑦ 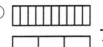 $\dfrac{1}{2}$ ___(>, < or =)___ $\dfrac{1}{4}$

⑧ 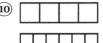 $\dfrac{4}{7}$ ___(>, < or =)___ $\dfrac{2}{5}$

⑨ $\dfrac{4}{10}$ ___(>, < or =)___ $\dfrac{2}{3}$

⑩ $\dfrac{2}{4}$ ___(>, < or =)___ $\dfrac{3}{6}$

⑪ $\dfrac{6}{8}$ ___(>, < or =)___ $\dfrac{1}{2}$

⑫ 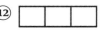 $\dfrac{1}{3}$ ___(>, < or =)___ $\dfrac{2}{4}$

⑬ $\dfrac{8}{10}$ ___(>, < or =)___ $\dfrac{4}{5}$

⑭ $\dfrac{1}{2}$ ___(>, < or =)___ $\dfrac{2}{5}$

Day 40
Mixed Numbers

Name: _____

Score:

Problems 1-5: *Shade the shapes to represents each fraction. (You may not need all the shapes to represent the fraction).*

① $4\frac{1}{2}$

② $6\frac{2}{3}$

③ $2\frac{5}{6}$

④ $\frac{1}{4}$

⑤ $3\frac{1}{3}$

Problems 6-10: *Write a fraction to represent the amount of shaded shapes.*

⑥ _____

⑦ _____

⑧ _____

⑨ _____

⑩ _____

Name: _____

Score:

Problems 1-6: *Is the fraction on the right greater than (>), less than (<), or equal to (=) the fraction on the left? Look at the shapes to help you decide.*

(1) $5\frac{1}{6}$ ____ (>, < or =) $3\frac{5}{6}$

(2) $2\frac{2}{3}$ ____ (>, < or =) $4\frac{2}{3}$

(3) $1\frac{3}{4}$ ____ (>, < or =) $1\frac{2}{4}$

(4) 4 ____ (>, < or =) $2\frac{1}{2}$

(5) $1\frac{1}{8}$ ____ (>, < or =) $\frac{7}{8}$

(6) $3\frac{2}{4}$ ____ (>, < or =) $2\frac{2}{4}$

Problems 7-14: *Decided if the fraction on the right is greater than (>), less than (<), or equal to (=) the fraction on the left. Draw your own shapes to help figure out the answer. .*

(7) $3\frac{4}{5}$ ____ (>, < or =) $6\frac{1}{3}$

(8) $3\frac{2}{3}$ ____ (>, < or =) $3\frac{2}{5}$

(9) $2\frac{1}{2}$ ____ (>, < or =) $1\frac{3}{4}$

(10) $2\frac{2}{4}$ ____ (>, < or =) $2\frac{1}{3}$

(11) $3\frac{5}{6}$ ____ (>, < or =) $5\frac{1}{8}$

(12) $\frac{3}{5}$ ____ (>, < or =) $2\frac{1}{5}$

(13) $8\frac{1}{8}$ ____ (>, < or =) $4\frac{1}{2}$

(14) $5\frac{4}{6}$ ____ (>, < or =) $5\frac{2}{3}$

Day 42

> < =

Name: _____

Problems 1-4: *Is the fraction on the right greater than (>), less than (<), or equal to (=) the fraction on the left? Look at the shapes to help you decide. Draw your own shapes if it helps you figure out the answer.*

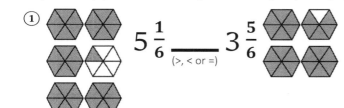

① $5\frac{1}{6}$ _____ $3\frac{5}{6}$
(>, < or =)

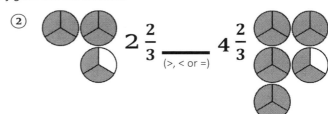

② $2\frac{2}{3}$ _____ $4\frac{2}{3}$
(>, < or =)

③ $3\frac{4}{5}$ _____ $6\frac{1}{3}$
(>, < or =)

④ $3\frac{2}{3}$ _____ $3\frac{2}{5}$
(>, < or =)

Problems 5-6: *Write the fractions in order from smallest to largest.*

⑤ $1\frac{2}{3}$ $\quad$ $3\frac{4}{5}$ $\quad$ $\frac{7}{8}$ $\quad$ $6\frac{3}{4}$ $\quad$ $3\frac{1}{2}$ $\quad$ $4\frac{1}{8}$ $\quad$ $6\frac{1}{3}$

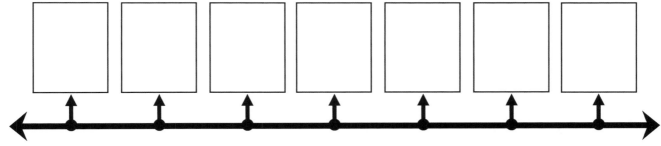

⑥ $4\frac{1}{2}$ $\quad$ $5\frac{1}{3}$ $\quad$ $4\frac{4}{5}$ $\quad$ $3\frac{2}{5}$ $\quad$ 4 $\quad$ $5\frac{1}{6}$ $\quad$ $3\frac{5}{6}$

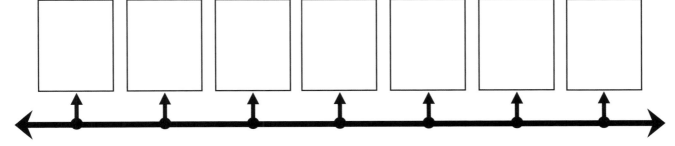

Day 43

Adding Fractions

Name: _____

Problems 1-6: *Shade the third image and then write the correct numerator to make the answer true.*

① $\dfrac{3}{8} + \dfrac{3}{8} = \dfrac{}{8}$

② $\dfrac{2}{5} + \dfrac{1}{5} = \dfrac{}{5}$

③ $\dfrac{4}{10} + \dfrac{3}{10} = \dfrac{}{10}$

④ $\dfrac{2}{6} + \dfrac{2}{6} = \dfrac{}{6}$

⑤ $\dfrac{1}{4} + \dfrac{2}{4} = \dfrac{}{4}$

⑥ $\dfrac{1}{3} + \dfrac{1}{3} = \dfrac{}{3}$

Problems 7-10: *Shade the three images and then write the correct numerator to make each answer true.*

⑦ $\dfrac{1}{3} + \dfrac{1}{3} = \dfrac{}{3}$

⑧ $\dfrac{3}{5} + \dfrac{1}{5} = \dfrac{}{5}$

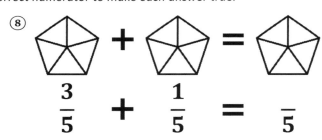

⑨ $\dfrac{5}{12} + \dfrac{4}{12} = \dfrac{}{12}$

⑩ $\dfrac{2}{6} + \dfrac{2}{6} = \dfrac{}{6}$

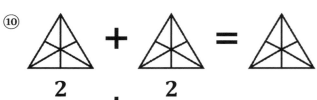

Day 44
Adding Fractions

Name: _____

Problems 1-4: *Shade the three images and then write the correct fraction to make each answer true.*

① $\dfrac{1}{6} + \dfrac{2}{6} = \ —$

② $\dfrac{2}{4} + \dfrac{2}{4} = \ —$

③ $\dfrac{10}{16} + \dfrac{3}{16} = \ —$

④ $\dfrac{2}{8} + \dfrac{3}{8} = \ —$

Problems 5-19: *Add each set of fractions.*

⑤ $\dfrac{3}{9} + \dfrac{4}{9} =$

⑥ $\dfrac{2}{5} + \dfrac{2}{5} =$

⑦ $\dfrac{1}{6} + \dfrac{4}{6} =$

⑧ $\dfrac{7}{15} + \dfrac{4}{15} =$

⑨ $\dfrac{2}{3} + \dfrac{1}{3} =$

⑩ $\dfrac{3}{8} + \dfrac{3}{8} =$

⑪ $\dfrac{7}{10} + \dfrac{4}{10} =$

⑫ $\dfrac{2}{7} + \dfrac{4}{7} =$

⑬ $\dfrac{2}{4} + \dfrac{1}{4} =$

⑭ $\dfrac{2}{6} + \dfrac{3}{6} =$

⑮ $\dfrac{4}{9} + \dfrac{2}{9} =$

⑯ $\dfrac{2}{5} + \dfrac{3}{5} =$

⑰ $\dfrac{1}{11} + \dfrac{1}{11} =$

⑱ $\dfrac{2}{8} + \dfrac{2}{8} =$

⑲ $\dfrac{3}{7} + \dfrac{3}{7} =$

Day 45

Subtracting Fractions

Score:

Problems 1-6: *Shade the third image and then write the correct numerator to make each answer true.*

①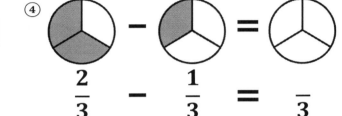

$$\frac{4}{5} - \frac{2}{5} = \frac{}{5}$$

②

$$\frac{2}{4} - \frac{1}{4} = \frac{}{4}$$

③

$$\frac{7}{8} - \frac{3}{8} = \frac{}{8}$$

④

$$\frac{2}{3} - \frac{1}{3} = \frac{}{3}$$

⑤

$$\frac{10}{10} - \frac{7}{10} = \frac{}{10}$$

⑥

$$\frac{4}{6} - \frac{2}{6} = \frac{}{6}$$

Problems 7-10: *Shade the three images and then write the correct numerator to make each answer true.*

⑦

$$\frac{3}{4} - \frac{1}{4} = \frac{}{4}$$

⑧

$$\frac{6}{8} - \frac{3}{8} = \frac{}{8}$$

⑨

$$\frac{4}{5} - \frac{1}{5} = \frac{}{5}$$

⑩

$$\frac{3}{6} - \frac{1}{6} = \frac{}{6}$$

Day 46
Subtracting Fractions

Name: _____

Score:

Problems 1-4: *Shade the three images and then write the correct fraction to make each answer true.*

① $\dfrac{2}{6} - \dfrac{1}{6} = \dfrac{}{}$

② $\dfrac{2}{4} - \dfrac{2}{4} = \dfrac{}{}$

③ $\dfrac{10}{16} - \dfrac{3}{16} = \dfrac{}{}$

④ $\dfrac{5}{8} - \dfrac{2}{8} = \dfrac{}{}$

Problems 5-9: *Subtract each set of fractions.*

⑤ $\dfrac{4}{6} - \dfrac{1}{6} =$

⑥ $\dfrac{5}{9} - \dfrac{1}{9} =$

⑦ $\dfrac{4}{5} - \dfrac{3}{5} =$

⑧ $\dfrac{8}{10} - \dfrac{4}{10} =$

⑨ $\dfrac{11}{12} - \dfrac{2}{12} =$

⑩ $\dfrac{7}{8} - \dfrac{3}{8} =$

⑪ $\dfrac{3}{4} - \dfrac{2}{4} =$

⑫ $\dfrac{5}{7} - \dfrac{3}{7} =$

⑬ $\dfrac{2}{3} - \dfrac{1}{3} =$

⑭ $\dfrac{13}{16} - \dfrac{2}{16} =$

⑮ $\dfrac{7}{10} - \dfrac{5}{10} =$

⑯ $\dfrac{2}{5} - \dfrac{1}{5} =$

⑰ $\dfrac{5}{6} - \dfrac{4}{6} =$

⑱ $\dfrac{5}{8} - \dfrac{2}{8} =$

⑲ $\dfrac{8}{9} - \dfrac{1}{9} =$

Name: _____

Score:

Problems 1-7: *Add each set of mixed fractions.*

①

$3\dfrac{5}{8}$ **+** $1\dfrac{1}{8}$ **=** _____

②

3 **+** $1\dfrac{3}{4}$ **=** _____

③

$3\dfrac{1}{3}$ **+** $2\dfrac{2}{3}$ **=** _____

④

$2\dfrac{1}{2}$ **+** 3 **=** _____

⑤

$2\dfrac{2}{6}$ **+** $\dfrac{3}{6}$ **=** _____

⑥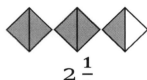

$2\dfrac{1}{4}$ **+** $2\dfrac{2}{4}$ **=** _____

⑦

1 **+** $2\dfrac{1}{2}$ **=** _____

Day 48
Adding Mixed Numbers

Name: _____

Score:

Problems 1-4: *Shade the images to represent each fraction, then add each set of fractions.*

①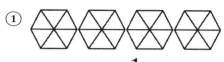

$3\frac{1}{6}$ **+** 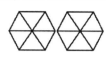 2 **=** ____

②

1 **+** $\frac{1}{2}$ **=** ____

③

$1\frac{2}{5}$ **+**  $2\frac{2}{5}$ **=** ____

④

2 **+** 2 **=** ____

Problems 5-16: *Add each set of fractions*

⑤ $5\frac{2}{4} + 3\frac{1}{4} =$

⑥ $4\frac{3}{6} + 2\frac{2}{6} =$

⑦ $1\frac{1}{3} + 7\frac{1}{3} =$

⑧ $2\frac{2}{7} + 3 =$

⑨ $6\frac{2}{5} + 5\frac{2}{5} =$

⑩ $1\frac{3}{16} + 4\frac{7}{16} =$

⑪ $2\frac{1}{4} + 2\frac{1}{4} =$

⑫ $5\frac{2}{8} + 1\frac{3}{8} =$

⑬ $8 + 4\frac{1}{2} =$

⑭ $2\frac{2}{7} + 3\frac{3}{7} =$

⑮ $4\frac{2}{9} + 1\frac{6}{9} =$

⑯ $3\frac{3}{10} + 3\frac{3}{10} =$

Name: _____

Score:

Problems 1-7: *Add each set of mixed fractions.*

①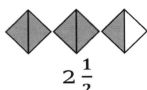

$2\dfrac{1}{2}$ + 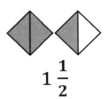 $1\dfrac{1}{2}$ = _____

②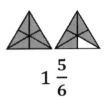

$1\dfrac{5}{6}$ + 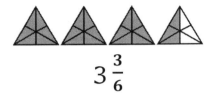 $3\dfrac{3}{6}$ = _____

③

$2\dfrac{1}{4}$ +  $2\dfrac{3}{4}$ = _____

④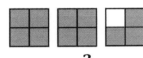

$3\dfrac{1}{2}$ + $3\dfrac{1}{2}$ = _____

⑤

$3\dfrac{2}{3}$ + $\dfrac{2}{3}$ = _____

⑥

$1\dfrac{5}{6}$ + $1\dfrac{4}{6}$ = _____

⑦

$1\dfrac{3}{8}$ + 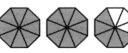 $2\dfrac{5}{8}$ = _____

Day 50

Adding Mixed Numbers

Name: _____

Problems 1-4: *Shade the images to represent each fraction, then add each set of fractions.*

① 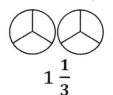 $1\frac{1}{3}$ **+**  $3\frac{2}{3}$ **=** ____

② 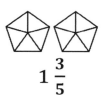 $2\frac{3}{4}$ **+** $\frac{3}{4}$ **=** ____

③ 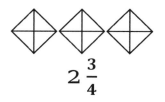 $1\frac{3}{5}$ **+** 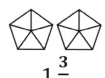 $1\frac{3}{5}$ **=** ____

④ 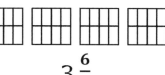 $3\frac{6}{8}$ **+**  $3\frac{7}{8}$ **=** ____

Problems 5-16: *Add each set of fractions*

⑤ $1\frac{2}{4} + 6\frac{3}{4} =$ ⑥ $4\frac{4}{7} + 2\frac{5}{7} =$ ⑦ $1\frac{2}{3} + \frac{1}{3} =$

⑧ $2\frac{1}{2} + 2\frac{1}{2} =$ ⑨ $6\frac{5}{9} + 5\frac{5}{9} =$ ⑩ $7\frac{11}{12} + 3\frac{8}{12} =$

⑪ $6\frac{4}{5} + 2\frac{3}{5} =$ ⑫ $1\frac{2}{8} + 5\frac{6}{8} =$ ⑬ $2\frac{2}{3} + 9\frac{2}{3} =$

⑭ $4\frac{4}{6} + 8\frac{3}{6} =$ ⑮ $1\frac{1}{2} + 1\frac{1}{2} =$ ⑯ $3\frac{3}{4} + 6\frac{3}{4} =$

Name: _____

Score:

Problems 1-27: *Add each set of fractions*

① $5\frac{3}{7} + 3\frac{3}{7} =$

② $4\frac{1}{3} + 7\frac{2}{3} =$

③ $8\frac{1}{2} + 2\frac{1}{2} =$

④ $2\frac{1}{9} + 1\frac{5}{9} =$

⑤ $6\frac{2}{4} + 3\frac{3}{4} =$

⑥ $1\frac{2}{5} + 1\frac{4}{5} =$

⑦ $4\frac{3}{8} + 4\frac{6}{8} =$

⑧ $2\frac{4}{8} + 3\frac{1}{8} =$

⑨ $9\frac{2}{6} + 7\frac{4}{6} =$

⑩ $5\frac{4}{7} + 2\frac{2}{7} =$

⑪ $7\frac{1}{2} + 2\frac{1}{2} =$

⑫ $4\frac{1}{5} + 3\frac{2}{5} =$

⑬ $8\frac{3}{4} + 5\frac{3}{4} =$

⑭ $6\frac{2}{7} + 6\frac{5}{7} =$

⑮ $2\frac{3}{5} + 2\frac{3}{5} =$

⑯ $7\frac{1}{2} + 1\frac{1}{2} =$

⑰ $4\frac{2}{3} + \frac{1}{3} =$

⑱ $1\frac{5}{12} + 5\frac{5}{12} =$

⑲ $4\frac{2}{7} + 2\frac{3}{7} =$

⑳ $8\frac{1}{2} + 1\frac{1}{2} =$

㉑ $5\frac{1}{3} + 5\frac{2}{3} =$

㉒ $\frac{6}{9} + 3\frac{4}{9} =$

㉓ $6\frac{4}{5} + 2\frac{3}{5} =$

㉔ $3\frac{2}{4} + 6\frac{1}{4} =$

㉕ $7\frac{4}{8} + 5\frac{6}{8} =$

㉖ $3\frac{4}{6} + 8\frac{2}{6} =$

㉗ $4\frac{1}{3} + 4\frac{1}{3} =$

Name: _____

Score:

Problems 1-7: *Subtract each set of fractions*

①

$$2\frac{1}{2} \qquad - \qquad 1\frac{1}{2} \qquad = \underline{\quad}$$

②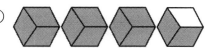

$$3\frac{2}{3} \qquad - \qquad 1\frac{1}{3} \qquad = \underline{\quad}$$

③

$$3\frac{4}{5} \qquad - \qquad \frac{2}{5} \qquad = \underline{\quad}$$

④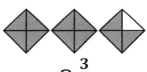

$$2\frac{3}{4} \qquad - \qquad 2\frac{1}{4} \qquad = \underline{\quad}$$

⑤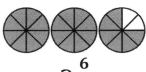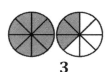

$$3\frac{6}{8} \qquad - \qquad 1\frac{3}{8} \qquad = \underline{\quad}$$

⑥

$$1\frac{1}{2} \qquad - \qquad 1\frac{1}{2} \qquad = \underline{\quad}$$

⑦

$$2\frac{5}{10} \qquad - \qquad 1\frac{1}{10} \qquad = \underline{\quad}$$

Day 53

Subtracting Mixed Numbers

Name: _____

Score:

Problems 1-4: *Shade the images to represent each fraction, then subtract each set of fractions.*

①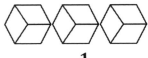

$$2\frac{1}{3} \qquad - \qquad 1\frac{1}{3} \qquad = \underline{\quad}$$

②

$$1\frac{3}{4} \qquad - \qquad 1\frac{1}{4} \qquad = \underline{\quad}$$

③

$$3\frac{5}{6} \qquad - \qquad 1\frac{3}{6} \qquad = \underline{\quad}$$

④

$$1\frac{4}{5} \qquad - \qquad 1\frac{2}{5} \qquad = \underline{\quad}$$

Problems 5-16: *Subtract each set of fractions.*

⑤ $8\frac{6}{7} - 5\frac{3}{7} =$ ⑥ $9\frac{3}{4} - 3\frac{1}{4} =$ ⑦ $4\frac{5}{8} - 3\frac{2}{8} =$

⑧ $6\frac{1}{3} - 2\frac{1}{3} =$ ⑨ $3\frac{6}{9} - 1\frac{4}{9} =$ ⑩ $8\frac{3}{5} - 4\frac{3}{5} =$

⑪ $7\frac{7}{8} - 1\frac{4}{8} =$ ⑫ $2\frac{4}{5} - \frac{3}{5} =$ ⑬ $5\frac{8}{10} - 3\frac{4}{10} =$

⑭ $6\frac{2}{4} - 4\frac{2}{4} =$ ⑮ $3\frac{2}{7} - 1\frac{1}{7} =$ ⑯ $8\frac{5}{6} - 2\frac{3}{6} =$

Name: _____

Score:

Problems 1-7: *Subtract each set of fractions*

① 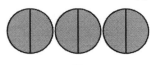   —   

3 — $2\frac{1}{2}$ = _____

② 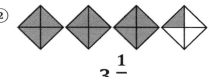   —

$3\frac{1}{4}$ — $1\frac{3}{4}$ = _____

③ 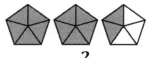   —

$2\frac{2}{5}$ — $\frac{3}{5}$ = _____

④    —   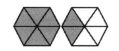

3 — $1\frac{2}{6}$ = _____

⑤    —

$3\frac{1}{3}$ — $\frac{1}{3}$ = _____

⑥   —   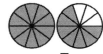

$1\frac{4}{8}$ — $\frac{6}{8}$ = _____

⑦ 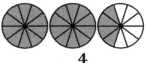   —

$2\frac{4}{10}$ — $1\frac{7}{10}$ = _____

Day 55
Subtracting Mixed Numbers

Name: _____

Problems 1-4: *Shade the images to represent each fraction, then subtract each set of fractions.*

①

$3\frac{2}{5}$ — $1\frac{3}{5}$ = _____

②

2 — $1\frac{2}{4}$ = _____

③ ▲▲▲ ▲

$2\frac{1}{3}$ — $\frac{2}{3}$ = _____

④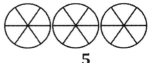

$2\frac{5}{6}$ — $2\frac{3}{6}$ = _____

Problems 5-16: *Subtract each set of fractions.*

⑤ $5\frac{2}{6} - 3\frac{3}{6} =$ ⑥ $4\frac{1}{4} - 1\frac{2}{4} =$ ⑦ $9 - 2\frac{1}{2} =$

⑧ $3\frac{1}{5} - \frac{3}{5} =$ ⑨ $8\frac{3}{7} - 7\frac{5}{7} =$ ⑩ $6\frac{1}{4} - 1\frac{3}{4} =$

⑪ $9\frac{5}{9} - 1\frac{8}{9} =$ ⑫ $5 - 2\frac{2}{3} =$ ⑬ $8\frac{1}{6} - 6\frac{5}{6} =$

⑭ $7\frac{2}{4} - 2\frac{3}{4} =$ ⑮ $2\frac{3}{8} - 1\frac{7}{8} =$ ⑯ $12\frac{1}{5} - 5\frac{3}{5} =$

Day 56
Subtracting Mixed Numbers

Name: _____

Score:

Problems 1-27: *Subtract each set of fractions.*

① $7\frac{3}{5} - 1\frac{4}{5} =$

② $6\frac{1}{2} - 2\frac{1}{2} =$

③ $2\frac{4}{7} - \frac{6}{7} =$

④ $6\frac{2}{3} - 4\frac{1}{3} =$

⑤ $8\frac{5}{9} - 2\frac{1}{9} =$

⑥ $3\frac{2}{8} - 1\frac{5}{8} =$

⑦ $4\frac{1}{4} - 3\frac{3}{4} =$

⑧ $8\frac{5}{6} - 5\frac{3}{6} =$

⑨ $9 - 3\frac{1}{4} =$

⑩ $8\frac{3}{9} - 4\frac{7}{9} =$

⑪ $3\frac{6}{7} - 1\frac{4}{7} =$

⑫ $5\frac{6}{10} - 3\frac{8}{10} =$

⑬ $5\frac{2}{7} - 3\frac{2}{7} =$

⑭ $6 - 2\frac{1}{2} =$

⑮ $4\frac{3}{5} - 1\frac{2}{5} =$

⑯ $2\frac{2}{4} - 1\frac{3}{4} =$

⑰ $7\frac{1}{8} - 2\frac{7}{8} =$

⑱ $11\frac{1}{3} - 7 =$

⑲ $8\frac{3}{6} - 3\frac{5}{6} =$

⑳ $3\frac{2}{9} - \frac{5}{9} =$

㉑ $6\frac{1}{5} - 1\frac{3}{5} =$

㉒ $8\frac{1}{3} - 6\frac{1}{3} =$

㉓ $9\frac{6}{7} - 1\frac{5}{7} =$

㉔ $9 - 2\frac{4}{7} =$

㉕ $8\frac{1}{5} - 7\frac{3}{5} =$

㉖ $3\frac{3}{4} - 1\frac{3}{4} =$

㉗ $6\frac{2}{6} - 4\frac{5}{6} =$

Name: _____

Problems 1-4: Shade the circle with the correct answer.

1.
Ⓐ 8:00
Ⓑ 5:00
Ⓒ 12:00
Ⓓ 3:00

2.
Ⓐ 7:00
Ⓑ 11:00
Ⓒ 1:00
Ⓓ 12:00

3.
Ⓐ 6:00
Ⓑ 10:00
Ⓒ 2:00
Ⓓ 5:00

4.
Ⓐ 4:00
Ⓑ 5:00
Ⓒ 11:00
Ⓓ 1:00

Problems 5-8: Write the correct time on the line beneath each clock.

5. _____
6. _____
7. _____
8. _____

Problems 9-12: Draw hands on each clock so they represent the corresponding times.

9. __1:00__
10. __4:00__
11. __11:00__
12. __2:00__

Name: _____

Problems 1-4: Shade the circle with the correct answer.

1. Ⓐ 11:00
    Ⓑ 3:00
    Ⓒ 4:00
    Ⓓ 7:00

2. Ⓐ 10:00
    Ⓑ 11:00
    Ⓒ 5:00
    Ⓓ 2:00

3. Ⓐ 12:00
    Ⓑ 7:00
    Ⓒ 8:00
    Ⓓ 6:00

4. Ⓐ 8:00
    Ⓑ 9:00
    Ⓒ 7:00
    Ⓓ 10:00

Problems 5-8: Write the correct time on the line beneath each clock.

5. _____   6. _____   7. _____   8. _____

Problems 9-12: Draw hands on each clock so they represent the corresponding times.

9. __6:00__   10. __11:00__   11. __12:00__   12. __3:00__

Name: _____

Problems 1-4: Shade the circle with the correct answer.

1. Ⓐ 12:00
   Ⓑ 10:00
   Ⓒ 2:00
   Ⓓ 7:00

2. Ⓐ 3:00
   Ⓑ 4:00
   Ⓒ 1:00
   Ⓓ 8:00

3. Ⓐ 1:00
   Ⓑ 11:00
   Ⓒ 5:00
   Ⓓ 6:00

4. Ⓐ 1:00
   Ⓑ 2:00
   Ⓒ 3:00
   Ⓓ 10:00

Problems 5-8: Write the correct time on the line beneath each clock.

5. _____

6. _____

7. _____

8. _____

Problems 9-12: Draw hands on each clock so they represent the corresponding times.

9. 8:00

10. 11:00

11. 6:00

12. 10:00

Name: _____

Problems 1-4: Shade the circle with the correct answer.

1.
Ⓐ 5:00
Ⓑ 1:00
Ⓒ 9:00
Ⓓ 3:00

2.
Ⓐ 2:00
Ⓑ 12:00
Ⓒ 4:00
Ⓓ 1:00

3.
Ⓐ 5:00
Ⓑ 6:00
Ⓒ 3:00
Ⓓ 4:00

4.
Ⓐ 2:00
Ⓑ 8:00
Ⓒ 7:00
Ⓓ 10:00

Problems 5-8: Write the correct time on the line beneath each clock.

5. _____

6. _____

7. _____

8. _____

Problems 9-12: Draw hands on each clock so they represent the corresponding times.

9. __2:00__

10. __6:00__

11. __10:00__

12. __3:00__

Day 61

Quarter Hours

Name: _____

Score:

Problems 1-4: Shade the circle with the correct answer.

1. Ⓐ 12:45
    Ⓑ 1:30
    Ⓒ 1:15
    Ⓓ 12:30

2. Ⓐ 3:45
    Ⓑ 3:15
    Ⓒ 9:15
    Ⓓ 2:45

3. Ⓐ 7:15
    Ⓑ 4:15
    Ⓒ 3:15
    Ⓓ 6:15

4. Ⓐ 7:00
    Ⓑ 6:00
    Ⓒ 12:00
    Ⓓ 5:00

Problems 5-8: Write the correct time on the line beneath each clock.

5. _____   6. _____   7. _____   8. _____

Problems 9-12: Draw hands on each clock so they represent the corresponding times.

9. __5:00__   10. __3:45__   11. __9:30__   12. __10:15__

© Libro Studio LLC 2020

Name: _____

Score:

Problems 1-4: Shade the circle with the correct answer.

1.
Ⓐ 3:45
Ⓑ 5:45
Ⓒ 4:45
Ⓓ 9:45

2.
Ⓐ 12:45
Ⓑ 9:45
Ⓒ 11:45
Ⓓ 10:45

3.
Ⓐ 7:30
Ⓑ 6:45
Ⓒ 8:45
Ⓓ 8:30

4.
Ⓐ 6:30
Ⓑ 6:15
Ⓒ 3:30
Ⓓ 7:15

Problems 5-8: Write the correct time on the line beneath each clock.

5. _____

6. _____

7. _____

8. _____

Problems 9-12: Draw hands on each clock so they represent the corresponding times.

9. __5:30__

10. __11:15__

11. __1:45__

12. __3:45__

© Libro Studio LLC 2020

Name: _____

Problems 1-4: Shade the circle with the correct answer.

1.
Ⓐ 3:45
Ⓑ 4:15
Ⓒ 9:15
Ⓓ 2:45

2.
Ⓐ 4:45
Ⓑ 9:30
Ⓒ 11:45
Ⓓ 10:45

3.
Ⓐ 3:15
Ⓑ 2:15
Ⓒ 1:15
Ⓓ 12:15

4.
Ⓐ 4:30
Ⓑ 6:15
Ⓒ 6:30
Ⓓ 5:30

Problems 5-8: Write the correct time on the line beneath each clock.

5. _____

6. _____

7. _____

8. _____

Problems 9-12: Draw hands on each clock so they represent the corresponding times.

9. __6:00__

10. __8:15__

11. __11:45__

12. __2:30__

Name: _____

Score:

Problems 1-4: Shade the circle with the correct answer.

1. Ⓐ 11:15
    Ⓑ 12:15
    Ⓒ 3:00
    Ⓓ 1:15

2. Ⓐ 7:30
    Ⓑ 6:45
    Ⓒ 6:30
    Ⓓ 8:45

3. Ⓐ 9:30
    Ⓑ 6:45
    Ⓒ 6:30
    Ⓓ 5:45

4. Ⓐ 2:30
    Ⓑ 1:15
    Ⓒ 3:15
    Ⓓ 2:15

Problems 5-8: Write the correct time on the line beneath each clock.

5. _____

6. _____

7. _____

8. _____

Problems 9-12: Draw hands on each clock so they represent the corresponding times.

9. __12:15__

10. __4:30__

11. __9:45__

12. __7:00__

Name: _____

Score:

Problems 1-4: Shade the circle with the correct answer.

1. Ⓐ 6:45
    Ⓑ 9:30
    Ⓒ 8:45
    Ⓓ 5:45

2. Ⓐ 2:15
    Ⓑ 2:45
    Ⓒ 2:30
    Ⓓ 3:15

3. Ⓐ 6:45
    Ⓑ 12:30
    Ⓒ 11:30
    Ⓓ 6:00

4. Ⓐ 8:15
    Ⓑ 3:45
    Ⓒ 8:30
    Ⓓ 9:15

Problems 5-8: Write the correct time on the line beneath each clock.

5. _____   6. _____   7. _____   8. _____

Problems 9-12: Draw hands on each clock so they represent the corresponding times.

9. __1:30__   10. __4:00__   11. __9:15__   12. __12:45__

Name: _____

Score:

Problems 1-4: Shade the circle with the correct answer.

1. Ⓐ 6:45
    Ⓑ 9:30
    Ⓒ 9:00
    Ⓓ 5:45

2. Ⓐ 4:30
    Ⓑ 5:45
    Ⓒ 4:45
    Ⓓ 9:30

3. Ⓐ 11:15
    Ⓑ 12:30
    Ⓒ 12:15
    Ⓓ 3:00

4. Ⓐ 3:30
    Ⓑ 5:15
    Ⓒ 5:30
    Ⓓ 3:15

Problems 5-8: Write the correct time on the line beneath each clock.

5. _____ 6. _____ 7. _____ 8. _____

Problems 9-12: Draw hands on each clock so they represent the corresponding times.

9. __7:15__   10. __2:30__   11. __12:45__   12. __10:15__

Day 67

Quarter Hours

Name: _____

Score:

Problems 1-4: Shade the circle with the correct answer.

1. Ⓐ 10:45
   Ⓑ 11:45
   Ⓒ 9:45
   Ⓓ 12:45

2. Ⓐ 6:15
   Ⓑ 1:30
   Ⓒ 5:15
   Ⓓ 12:30

3. Ⓐ 12:30
   Ⓑ 6:00
   Ⓒ 12:15
   Ⓓ 12:00

4. Ⓐ 11:45
   Ⓑ 12:45
   Ⓒ 9:00
   Ⓓ 9:45

Problems 5-8: Write the correct time on the line beneath each clock.

5. _____

6. _____

7. _____

8. _____

Problems 9-12: Draw hands on each clock so they represent the corresponding times.

9. __8:15__

10. __4:30__

11. __7:15__

12. __3:45__

© Libro Studio LLC 2020

Name: _____

Score:

Problems 1-4: Shade the circle with the correct answer.

1. Ⓐ 5:30
    Ⓑ 9:30
    Ⓒ 6:30
    Ⓓ 5:45

2. Ⓐ 7:00
    Ⓑ 12:30
    Ⓒ 8:00
    Ⓓ 6:00

3. Ⓐ 12:15
    Ⓑ 1:15
    Ⓒ 12:15
    Ⓓ 3:15

4. Ⓐ 8:30
    Ⓑ 6:45
    Ⓒ 9:30
    Ⓓ 9:45

Problems 5-8: Write the correct time on the line beneath each clock.

5. _____

6. _____

7. _____

8. _____

Problems 9-12: Draw hands on each clock so they represent the corresponding times.

9. __3:45__

10. __11:15__

11. __9:30__

12. __5:15__

Name: _____

Problems 1-4: Shade the circle with the correct answer.

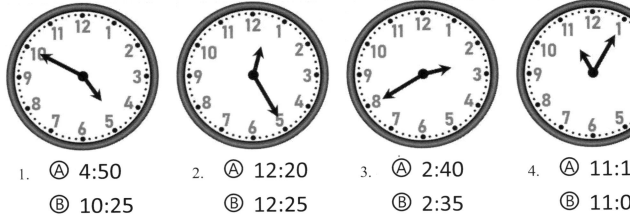

1. Ⓐ 4:50
   Ⓑ 10:25
   Ⓒ 5:50
   Ⓓ 5:45

2. Ⓐ 12:20
   Ⓑ 12:25
   Ⓒ 1:25
   Ⓓ 1:30

3. Ⓐ 2:40
   Ⓑ 2:35
   Ⓒ 3:40
   Ⓓ 3:45

4. Ⓐ 11:10
   Ⓑ 11:05
   Ⓒ 11:00
   Ⓓ 10:05

Problems 5-8: Write the correct time on the line beneath each clock.

5. _____   6. _____   7. _____   8. _____

Problems 9-12: Draw hands on each clock so they represent the corresponding times.

9. __9:20__   10. __1:35__   11. __12:50__   12. __6:40__

Day 70

Name: _____

Score: _____

Problems 1-4: Shade the circle with the correct answer.

1. Ⓐ 2:50
   Ⓑ 10:20
   Ⓒ 10:10
   Ⓓ 2:45

2. Ⓐ 12:30
   Ⓑ 6:05
   Ⓒ 1:30
   Ⓓ 1:15

3. Ⓐ 7:40
   Ⓑ 6:40
   Ⓒ 8:40
   Ⓓ 8:35

4. Ⓐ 2:25
   Ⓑ 3:25
   Ⓒ 4:15
   Ⓓ 5:15

Problems 5-8: Write the correct time on the line beneath each clock.

5. _____

6. _____

7. _____

8. _____

Problems 9-12: Draw hands on each clock so they represent the corresponding times.

9. __11:50__

10. __4:10__

11. __7:45__

12. __2:35__

Name: _____

Score:

Problems 1-4: Shade the circle with the correct answer.

1. Ⓐ 8:20
    Ⓑ 8:05
    Ⓒ 8:25
    Ⓓ 8:10

2. Ⓐ 1:30
    Ⓑ 1:25
    Ⓒ 2:25
    Ⓓ 2:30

3. Ⓐ 6:45
    Ⓑ 6:35
    Ⓒ 7:40
    Ⓓ 7:45

4. Ⓐ 4:10
    Ⓑ 5:50
    Ⓒ 4:50
    Ⓓ 5:10

Problems 5-8: Write the correct time on the line beneath each clock.

5. _____   6. _____   7. _____   8. _____

Problems 9-12: Draw hands on each clock so they represent the corresponding times.

9. ___1:10___   10. ___8:20___   11. ___9:05___   12. ___4:50___

Day 72

Five Minutes

Name: _____

Problems 1-4: Shade the circle with the correct answer.

1. Ⓐ 2:55
    Ⓑ 11:15
    Ⓒ 11:30
    Ⓓ 3:55

2. Ⓐ 6:50
    Ⓑ 5:30
    Ⓒ 5:35
    Ⓓ 6:25

3. Ⓐ 3:40
    Ⓑ 8:15
    Ⓒ 4:40
    Ⓓ 8:20

4. Ⓐ 1:30
    Ⓑ 5:30
    Ⓒ 6:05
    Ⓓ 6:10

Problems 5-8: Write the correct time on the line beneath each clock.

5. _____

6. _____

7. _____

8. _____

Problems 9-12: Draw hands on each clock so they represent the corresponding times.

9. ___6:30___

10. ___11:15___

11. ___2:35___

12. ___7:55___

Day 73

Five Minutes

Name: _____

Problems 1-4: Shade the circle with the correct answer.

1. Ⓐ 6:40
   Ⓑ 6:30
   Ⓒ 6:35
   Ⓓ 7:35

2. Ⓐ 9:50
   Ⓑ 9:55
   Ⓒ 11:45
   Ⓓ 8:55

3. Ⓐ 5:45
   Ⓑ 5:30
   Ⓒ 6:45
   Ⓓ 9:30

4. Ⓐ 10:50
   Ⓑ 5:10
   Ⓒ 10:25
   Ⓓ 5:10

Problems 5-8: Write the correct time on the line beneath each clock.

5. _____

6. _____

7. _____

8. _____

Problems 9-12: Draw hands on each clock so they represent the corresponding times.

9. 12:30

10. 8:55

11. 5:25

12. 1:05

Name: _____

Problems 1-4: Shade the circle with the correct answer.

1. Ⓐ 9:15
    Ⓑ 9:30
    Ⓒ 3:45
    Ⓓ 10:15

2. Ⓐ 11:00
    Ⓑ 2:20
    Ⓒ 2:10
    Ⓓ 2:00

3. Ⓐ 10:25
    Ⓑ 9:25
    Ⓒ 9:50
    Ⓓ 10:50

4. Ⓐ 11:05
    Ⓑ 1:55
    Ⓒ 11:10
    Ⓓ 12:55

Problems 5-8: Write the correct time on the line beneath each clock.

5. _____   6. _____   7. _____   8. _____

Problems 9-12: Draw hands on each clock so they represent the corresponding times.

9. ____4:45____   10. ____2:15____   11. ____10:40____   12. ____8:50____

Name: _____

Problems 1-4: Shade the circle with the correct answer.

1. Ⓐ 6:35
    Ⓑ 7:30
    Ⓒ 5:35
    Ⓓ 12:50

2. Ⓐ 8:10
    Ⓑ 2:40
    Ⓒ 3:40
    Ⓓ 8:30

3. Ⓐ 2:15
    Ⓑ 1:55
    Ⓒ 2:55
    Ⓓ 11:10

4. Ⓐ 10:20
    Ⓑ 10:15
    Ⓒ 4:50
    Ⓓ 4:15

Problems 5-8: Write the correct time on the line beneath each clock.

5. _____

6. _____

7. _____

8. _____

Problems 9-12: Draw hands on each clock so they represent the corresponding times.

9. ___5:45___

10. ___2:40___

11. ___3:25___

12. ___11:20___

Day 76

Five Minutes

Name: _____

Problems 1-4: Shade the circle with the correct answer.

1.
   Ⓐ 7:20
   Ⓑ 7:30
   Ⓒ 4:07
   Ⓓ 4:20

2.
   Ⓐ 8:20
   Ⓑ 8:25
   Ⓒ 8:10
   Ⓓ 8:30

3.
   Ⓐ 11:25
   Ⓑ 12:30
   Ⓒ 12:25
   Ⓓ 11:35

4.
   Ⓐ 6:40
   Ⓑ 5:25
   Ⓒ 6:25
   Ⓓ 5:50

Problems 5-8: Write the correct time on the line beneath each clock.

5. _____

6. _____

7. _____

8. _____

Problems 9-12: Draw hands on each clock so they represent the corresponding times.

9. ____4:55____

10. ____3:40____

11. ____11:15____

12. ____12:00____

Day 77

Minutes

Name: _____

Score:

Problems 1-4: Shade the circle with the correct answer.

1. Ⓐ 1:12
    Ⓑ 1:02
    Ⓒ 1:05
    Ⓓ 12:02

2. Ⓐ 12:24
    Ⓑ 12:20
    Ⓒ 12:05
    Ⓓ 12:04

3. Ⓐ 6:06
    Ⓑ 6:05
    Ⓒ 6:07
    Ⓓ 6:10

4. Ⓐ 7:10
    Ⓑ 7:08
    Ⓒ 7:07
    Ⓓ 7:05

Problems 5-8: Write the correct time on the line beneath each clock.

5. _____   6. _____   7. _____   8. _____

Problems 9-12: Draw hands on each clock so they represent the corresponding times.

9. ___12:32___   10. ___12:47___   11. ___11:18___   12. ___1:18___

Day 78
Minutes

Name: _____

Score:

Problems 1-4: Shade the circle with the correct answer.

1. Ⓐ 10:30
    Ⓑ 10:32
    Ⓒ 10:33
    Ⓓ 7:50

2. Ⓐ 8:39
    Ⓑ 7:39
    Ⓒ 7:38
    Ⓓ 8:38

3. Ⓐ 5:25
    Ⓑ 5:43
    Ⓒ 5:44
    Ⓓ 5:35

4. Ⓐ 9:48
    Ⓑ 9:45
    Ⓒ 8:46
    Ⓓ 9:50

Problems 5-8: Write the correct time on the line beneath each clock.

5. _____   6. _____   7. _____   8. _____

Problems 9-12: Draw hands on each clock so they represent the corresponding times.

9. _____ 7:18 _____   10. _____ 7:26 _____   11. _____ 7:38 _____   12. _____ 7:46 _____

Name: _____

Problems 1-4: Shade the circle with the correct answer.

1. Ⓐ 10:15
   Ⓑ 10:14
   Ⓒ 10:13
   Ⓓ 10:12

2. Ⓐ 7:20
   Ⓑ 7:21
   Ⓒ 7:22
   Ⓓ 7:23

3. Ⓐ 7:25
   Ⓑ 7:30
   Ⓒ 7:39
   Ⓓ 7:38

4. Ⓐ 6:47
   Ⓑ 6:45
   Ⓒ 6:46
   Ⓓ 6:28

Problems 5-8: Write the correct time on the line beneath each clock.

5. _____

6. _____

7. _____

8. _____

Problems 9-12: Draw hands on each clock so they represent the corresponding times.

9. __2:36__

10. __9:17__

11. __7:13__

12. __4:17__

Name: _____

Problems 1-4: Shade the circle with the correct answer.

1. Ⓐ 8:02
   Ⓑ 8:01
   Ⓒ 8:03
   Ⓓ 8:10

2. Ⓐ 10:02
   Ⓑ 10:03
   Ⓒ 10:04
   Ⓓ 10:05

3. Ⓐ 5:02
   Ⓑ 5:03
   Ⓒ 6:06
   Ⓓ 5:06

4. Ⓐ 6:04
   Ⓑ 6:09
   Ⓒ 6:10
   Ⓓ 6:02

Problems 5-8: Write the correct time on the line beneath each clock.

5. _____

6. _____

7. _____

8. _____

Problems 9-12: Draw hands on each clock so they represent the corresponding times.

9. ___2:16___

10. ___4:18___

11. ___11:12___

12. ___10:48___

Name: _____

Score:

Problems 1-4: Shade the circle with the correct answer.

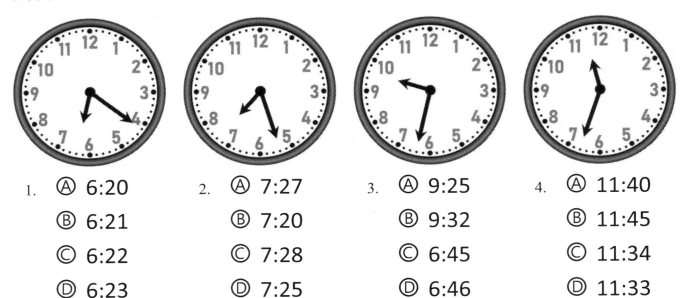

1. Ⓐ 6:20
   Ⓑ 6:21
   Ⓒ 6:22
   Ⓓ 6:23

2. Ⓐ 7:27
   Ⓑ 7:20
   Ⓒ 7:28
   Ⓓ 7:25

3. Ⓐ 9:25
   Ⓑ 9:32
   Ⓒ 6:45
   Ⓓ 6:46

4. Ⓐ 11:40
   Ⓑ 11:45
   Ⓒ 11:34
   Ⓓ 11:33

Problems 5-8: Write the correct time on the line beneath each clock.

5. _____

6. _____

7. _____

8. _____

Problems 9-12: Draw hands on each clock so they represent the corresponding times.

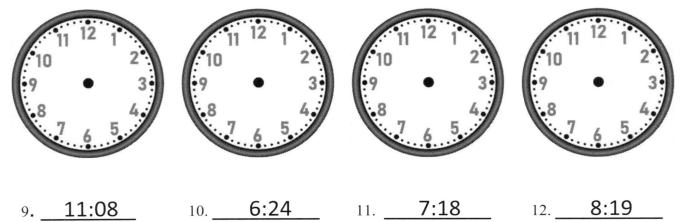

9. ___11:08___

10. ___6:24___

11. ___7:18___

12. ___8:19___

Day 82
Minutes

Name: _____

Score:

Problems 1-4: Shade the circle with the correct answer.

1. Ⓐ 12:24
    Ⓑ 12:25
    Ⓒ 11:24
    Ⓓ 11:23

2. Ⓐ 5:28
    Ⓑ 5:29
    Ⓒ 5:26
    Ⓓ 6:30

3. Ⓐ 9:25
    Ⓑ 9:32
    Ⓒ 9:50
    Ⓓ 9:12

4. Ⓐ 2:37
    Ⓑ 3:46
    Ⓒ 2:35
    Ⓓ 2:36

Problems 5-8: Write the correct time on the line beneath each clock.

5. _____ 6. _____ 7. _____ 8. _____

Problems 9-12: Draw hands on each clock so they represent the corresponding times.

9. ___1:18___   10. ___3:41___   11. ___4:57___   12. ___9:18___

Day 83

Minutes

Name: _____

Problems 1-4: Shade the circle with the correct answer.

1. Ⓐ 10:30
    Ⓑ 10:13
    Ⓒ 10:12
    Ⓓ 10:14

2. Ⓐ 5:17
    Ⓑ 5:16
    Ⓒ 5:15
    Ⓓ 5:14

3. Ⓐ 3:25
    Ⓑ 3:30
    Ⓒ 3:22
    Ⓓ 3:35

4. Ⓐ 5:29
    Ⓑ 6:29
    Ⓒ 7:29
    Ⓓ 5:30

Problems 5-8: Write the correct time on the line beneath each clock.

5. _____ 6. _____ 7. _____ 8. _____

Problems 9-12: Draw hands on each clock so they represent the corresponding times.

9. ___2:28___   10. ___12:17___   11. ___7:43___   12. ___8:13___

Name: _____

Problems 1-4: Shade the circle with the correct answer.

1.
  Ⓐ 5:24
  Ⓑ 5:21
  Ⓒ 5:18
  Ⓓ 5:27

2.
  Ⓐ 10:19
  Ⓑ 10:29
  Ⓒ 10:26
  Ⓓ 6:18

3.
  Ⓐ 10:25
  Ⓑ 10:30
  Ⓒ 10:50
  Ⓓ 10:37

4.
  Ⓐ 6:44
  Ⓑ 6:45
  Ⓒ 9:35
  Ⓓ 9:42

Problems 5-8: Write the correct time on the line beneath each clock.

5. _____

6. _____

7. _____

8. _____

Problems 9-12: Draw hands on each clock so they represent the corresponding times.

9. ____6:19____

10. ____12:28____

11. ____7:02____

12. ____3:43____

Name: _____

Problems 1-4: Shade the circle with the correct answer.

1. Ⓐ 7:56
   Ⓑ 7:55
   Ⓒ 6:56
   Ⓓ 6:58

2. Ⓐ 12:52
   Ⓑ 2:50
   Ⓒ 12:10
   Ⓓ 1:52

3. Ⓐ 6:55
   Ⓑ 6:54
   Ⓒ 6:50
   Ⓓ 7:54

4. Ⓐ 7:10
   Ⓑ 6:08
   Ⓒ 7:08
   Ⓓ 6:12

Problems 5-8: Write the correct time on the line beneath each clock.

5. _____ 6. _____ 7. _____ 8. _____

Problems 9-12: Draw hands on each clock so they represent the corresponding times.

9. __3:28__ 10. __10:29__ 11. __10:46__ 12. __9:11__

Name: _____

Problems 1-4: Shade the circle with the correct answer.

1.	Ⓐ 10:22	2.	Ⓐ 4:34	3.	Ⓐ 10:25	4.	Ⓐ 5:43
	Ⓑ 10:32		Ⓑ 4:33		Ⓑ 10:36		Ⓑ 5:45
	Ⓒ 10:35		Ⓒ 5:33		Ⓒ 10:37		Ⓒ 5:42
	Ⓓ 10:11		Ⓓ 5:44		Ⓓ 10:38		Ⓓ 5:51

Problems 5-8: Write the correct time on the line beneath each clock.

5. _____   6. _____   7. _____   8. _____

Problems 9-12: Draw hands on each clock so they represent the corresponding times.

9. __12:09__   10. __2:08__   11. __5:19__   12. __3:19__

Name: _____

Problems 1-4: Draw hands on each clock so they represent the corresponding times.

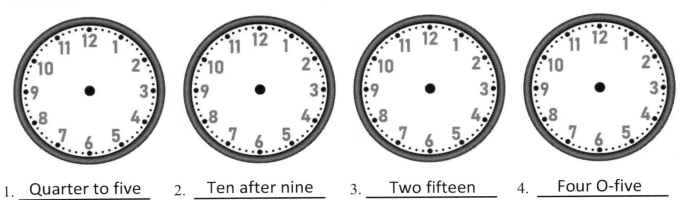

1. __Quarter to five__   2. __Ten after nine__   3. __Two fifteen__   4. __Four O-five__

Problems 5-8: Shade the circle with the correct answer.

5. Five to ten
Ⓐ 10:05
Ⓑ 10:55
Ⓒ 9:55
Ⓓ 5:10

6. Quarter after three
Ⓐ 3:45
Ⓑ 3:20
Ⓒ 3:30
Ⓓ 3:15

7. Eight forty-two
Ⓐ 8:42
Ⓑ 8:59
Ⓒ 8:40
Ⓓ 8:57

8. Four ten
Ⓐ 4:50
Ⓑ 4:05
Ⓒ 4:40
Ⓓ 4:10

Problems 9-12: Solve each word problem.

9. Jacobs flight left at 10:47 a.m. and landed at 2:15 p.m. How long was his flight?

10. Amanda's mom says she must go to bed at 9 pm. It is 7:40 p.m. now. How much time does she have before her bedtime?

11. Shannon played video games for 37 minutes. Ben played video games for 1 hour and 21 minutes. How much longer did Ben play than Shannon?

12. Pam left her house at 8:26 a.m. She went to the store, the bank, and got her hair cut. She did not get back home until 10:54 a.m. How long was she gone?

Name: _____

Score:

Problems 1-4: Draw hands on each clock so they represent the corresponding times.

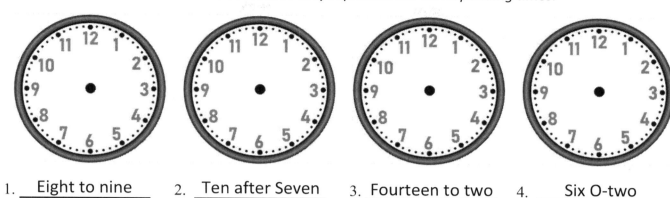

1. __Eight to nine__   2. __Ten after Seven__   3. __Fourteen to two__   4. __Six O-two__

Problems 5-8: Shade the circle with the correct answer.

5. Twenty to five	6. Five to eleven	7. Four thirty	8. Nine fifty-four
Ⓐ 4:40	Ⓐ 10:52	Ⓐ 3:40	Ⓐ 9:04
Ⓑ 5:40	Ⓑ 11:05	Ⓑ 4:30	Ⓑ 8:40
Ⓒ 4:20	Ⓒ 10:55	Ⓒ 4:13	Ⓒ 9:40
Ⓓ 5:20	Ⓓ 10:05	Ⓓ 4:57	Ⓓ 9:54

Problems 9-12: Solve each word problem.

9. Kyle arrived at the amusement park at 9:45 a.m. He did not leave until 6:19 p.m. How much time did he spend at the park?

10. Kyle had to wait in line for his favorite rollercoaster ride. He got in line at 11:43 a.m. and had to wait for 25 minutes before entering the ride. What time was it when he entered the ride?

11. Alex is babysitting his neighbors' kids. He started watching them at 4:10 p.m., and their parents did not come back until 7:55 p.m. How long was he babysitting?

12. Bella went to a parade. It started at 2 p.m. and did not end until 3:16 p.m. How long did the parade last?

Name: _____

Problems 1-4: Draw hands on each clock so they represent the corresponding times.

1. __Eight thirty-nine__   2. __Twenty after two__   3. _____Seven ten_____   4. __Twelve to nine__

Problems 5-8: Shade the circle with the correct answer.

5. Three O-six	6. Ten twenty-one	7. Ten after five	8. Fifteen to four
Ⓐ 6:03	Ⓐ 10:21	Ⓐ 5:50	Ⓐ 4:15
Ⓑ 3:36	Ⓑ 1:20	Ⓑ 10:05	Ⓑ 4:35
Ⓒ 3:06	Ⓒ 12:20	Ⓒ 4:50	Ⓒ 4:45
Ⓓ 6:33	Ⓓ 1:10	Ⓓ 5:10	Ⓓ 3:45

Problems 9-12: Solve each word problem.

9. Megan went to a birthday party at 11:30 a.m. Her dad came to pick her up from the party 4 hours and 45 minutes later. What time did she leave the party?

10. It started to rain at 10:35 a.m. and did not stop for 16 hours. What time did the rain finally stop?

11. Terry took her medicine at 9:30 a.m. She is supposed to take another dose 8 hours later. What time should the next dose be taken?

12. The fireworks show starts at sunset. It is currently 6:14 p.m. Sunset is not until 8:36 p.m. How much longer until the fireworks show begins?

Name: _____

Score:

Problems 1-4: Draw hands on each clock so they represent the corresponding times.

1. ___Seven fifteen___   2. ___Nine forty-two___   3. ___Ten past three___   4. ___Twenty to six___

Problems 5-8: Shade the circle with the correct answer.

5. Thirteen to one	6. Ten after twelve	7. Eight eleven	8. Twenty-five to one
Ⓐ 1:13	Ⓐ 1:10	Ⓐ 8:11	Ⓐ 1:25
Ⓑ 1:47	Ⓑ 12:10	Ⓑ 8:49	Ⓑ 12:35
Ⓒ 12:13	Ⓒ 10:53	Ⓒ 11:08	Ⓒ 12:45
Ⓓ 12:47	Ⓓ 10:22	Ⓓ 11:52	Ⓓ 1:45

Problems 9-12: Solve each word problem.

9. Pam goes to the pool at 3:05 p.m. and swims until 4:40 p.m. How long did she swim?

10. Nate's GPS says it will take him 50 minutes to drive to his grandma's house. He runs into slow traffic, so it takes 1 hour and 15 minutes instead. How much time did the slow traffic add to his drive?

11. Gavin is baking. He is supposed to roast the food for 2 hours, but forgot to set the timer when he put the food in. He thinks its been in for 25 minutes. How much longer does the food need to bake?

12. It is 3:15 p.m. now. What time should the food be taken out of the oven? (*Refer to the information in question 11 and the answer you found*)

Name: _____

Score:

Problems 1-4: *Write the value of each group.*

① $ _____

② $ _____

③ $ _____

④ $ _____

Problems 5-8: *Write the correct time on the line beneath each clock.*

⑤ _____

⑥ _____

⑦ _____

⑧ _____

Problems 9-11: *Add each set of fractions*

⑨ $5\frac{1}{6} + 1\frac{5}{6} =$

⑩ $2\frac{3}{4} + 3\frac{3}{4} =$

⑪ $1\frac{2}{7} + 4\frac{4}{7} =$

Day 92

Mixed Review

Name: _____

Score:

Problems 1-4: *Write the value of each group.*

① $ _____

② $ _____

③ $ _____

④ $ _____

Problems 5-8: *Write the correct time on the line beneath each clock.*

⑤ _____   ⑥ _____   ⑦ _____   ⑧ _____

Problems 9-11: *Add each set of fractions*

⑨ $6\frac{1}{2} - 3 =$ ⑩ $8\frac{1}{5} - 2\frac{3}{5} =$ ⑪ $4\frac{5}{10} - 3\frac{3}{10} =$

Name: _____

Problems 1-4: *Write the value of each group.*

① $ _____

② $ _____

③ $ _____

④ $ _____

Problems 5-8: *Write the correct time on the line beneath each clock.*

⑤ _____   ⑥ _____   ⑦ _____   ⑧ _____

Problems 9-11: *Add each set of fractions*

⑨ $2\frac{2}{4} + 5\frac{3}{4} =$ ⑩ $4\frac{4}{7} + 3\frac{5}{7} =$ ⑪ $1\frac{1}{3} + 1\frac{2}{3} =$

Day 94

Mixed Review

Name: _____

Score:

Problems 1-4: *Write the value of each group.*

① $ _____

② $ _____

③ $ _____

④ $ _____

Problems 5-8: *Write the correct time on the line beneath each clock.*

⑤ _____

⑥ _____

⑦ _____

⑧ _____

Problems 9-11: *Add each set of fractions*

⑨ $5\frac{4}{8} - 1\frac{5}{8} =$

⑩ $6\frac{1}{3} - 5\frac{2}{3} =$

⑪ $8\frac{9}{12} - 3\frac{8}{12} =$

Day 95

Mixed Review

Name: _____

Score:

Problems 1-4: *Write the value of each group.*

① $ _____

② $ _____

③ $ _____

④ $ _____

Problems 5-8: *Write the correct time on the line beneath each clock.*

⑤ _____   ⑥ _____   ⑦ _____   ⑧ _____

Problems 9-11: *Add each set of fractions*

⑨ $7\frac{1}{2} + \frac{1}{2} =$

⑩ $3\frac{3}{5} + 8\frac{3}{5} =$

⑪ $2\frac{5}{6} + 4\frac{3}{6} =$

Day 96
Mixed Review

Name: _____

Score:

Problems 1-4: *Write the value of each group.*

① $ _____

② $ _____

③ $ _____

④ $ _____

Problems 5-8: *Write the correct time on the line beneath each clock.*

⑤ _____   ⑥ _____   ⑦ _____   ⑧ _____

Problems 9-11: *Add each set of fractions*

⑨ $7\frac{2}{4} - 5\frac{1}{4} =$

⑩ $9\frac{2}{6} - 1\frac{5}{6} =$

⑪ $5\frac{2}{7} - 2\frac{3}{7} =$

© Libro Studio LLC 2020

Name: _____

Score:

Problems 1-4: *Write the value of each group.*

① $_____

② $_____

③ $_____

④ $_____

Problems 5-8: *Write the correct time on the line beneath each clock.*

⑤ _____ ⑥ _____ ⑦ _____ ⑧ _____

Problems 9-11: *Add each set of fractions*

⑨ $4\frac{4}{8} + 2\frac{6}{8} =$

⑩ $6\frac{1}{3} + 1\frac{1}{3} =$

⑪ $5\frac{7}{9} + 3\frac{6}{9} =$

Name: _____

Score:

Problems 1-4: *Write the value of each group.*

① $ _____

② $ _____

③ $ _____

④ $ _____

Problems 5-8: *Write the correct time on the line beneath each clock.*

⑤ _____

⑥ _____

⑦ _____

⑧ _____

Problems 9-11: *Add each set of fractions*

⑨ $4\frac{4}{5} - 4\frac{1}{5} =$

⑩ $9\frac{1}{4} - 5\frac{2}{4} =$

⑪ $8\frac{8}{10} - 1\frac{3}{10} =$

Name: _____

Score:

Problems 1-4: *Write the value of each group.*

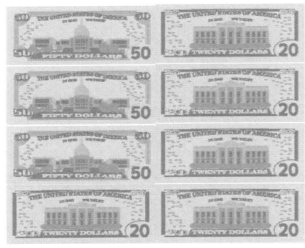

① $_____

② $_____

③ $_____

④ $_____

Problems 5-8: *Write the correct time on the line beneath each clock.*

⑤ _____

⑥ _____

⑦ _____

⑧ _____

Problems 9-11: *Add each set of fractions*

⑨ $5\frac{2}{5} + 2\frac{4}{5} =$

⑩ $1\frac{5}{9} + 1\frac{3}{9} =$

⑪ $3\frac{2}{4} + 6\frac{2}{4} =$

Day 100
Mixed Review

Name: _____

Score:

Problems 1-4: *Write the value of each group.*

① $ _____

② $ _____

③ $ _____

④ $ _____

Problems 5-8: *Write the correct time on the line beneath each clock.*

⑤ _____

⑥ _____

⑦ _____

⑧ _____

Problems 9-11: *Add each set of fractions*

⑨ $6\frac{4}{7} - 5\frac{6}{7} =$

⑩ $3\frac{5}{9} - 1\frac{5}{9} =$

⑪ $7\frac{1}{6} - 3\frac{3}{6} =$

Answers

Day 1:
1) Penny 2) Nickel 3) Dime
4) 1¢ 5) 5¢ 6) 10¢
7) 15¢ 8) 40¢ 9) 7¢ 10) 25¢
11) 20¢ 12) 36¢ 13) 58¢ 14) 51¢ 15) 92¢
16) 59¢ 17) 15¢ 18) 83¢ 19) 71¢ 20) 90¢

Day 2:
1) 8¢ 2) 11¢ 3) 16¢ 4) 16¢
5) 28¢ 6) 26¢ 7) 50¢ 8) 38¢
9) 17¢ 10) 67¢ 11) 59¢ 12) 41¢

Day 3:
1) A 2) A 3) B 4) B
5) D 6) C 7) C 8) C

Day 4:
1) 25¢ 2) 50¢ 3) 75¢ 4) 100¢
5) 56¢ 6) 50¢ 7) 85¢ 8) 57¢
9) 82¢ 10) 84¢

Day 5:
1) 85¢ 2) 60¢ 3) 62¢ 4) 80¢
5) 95¢ 6) 92¢ 7) 68¢ 8) 73¢

Day 6:
1) 41¢ 2) 62¢ 3) 81¢ 4) 92¢
5) 76¢ 6) 98¢ 7) 82¢ 8) 75¢
9) 87¢ 10) 66¢ 11) 79¢ 12) 90¢

Day 7:
1) 84¢ 2) 84¢ 3) 80¢ 4) 65¢
5) 63¢ 6) 78¢ 7) 88¢ 8) 77¢

Day 8:
1) 22¢ 2) 21¢ 3) 29¢ 4) 66¢ 5) 3¢
6) 74¢ 7) 15¢ 8) 10¢ 9) 32¢ 10) 47¢
11) 36¢ 12) 17¢ 13) 25¢ 14) 32¢ 15) 72¢

Day 9:
1) 3¢ 2) 96¢ 3) 8¢
4) 8 5) 18¢ 6) 69¢

Day 10:
1) $0.25 2) $0.50 3) $0.75 4) $1.00
5) $1.25 6) $1.50 7) $1.75 8) $2.00
9) $3.00 10) $2.50 11) $5.75 12) $7.25

Day 11:
1) $1.87 2) $4.22 3) $8.91 4) $12.40
5) $8.95 6) $1.52 7) $1.31 8) $1.87
9) $1.81 10) $2.14 11) $3.05 12) $4.20
13) $2.49 14) $3.39 15) $3.47

Day 12:
1) 1 2) 2 3) 25 4) 10
5) 1 6) 5 7) 12 8) 50
9) 3 10) 10 11) 35 12) 8
13) 50 14) 8 15) 9 16) 15

Day 13:
1) $3.39 2) $7.54 3) $0.71 4) $8.06
5) $0.56 6) $7.00 7) $7.71 8) $4.56
9) $5.27 10) $7.75 11) $1.83 12) $1.81

Day 14:
1) $5.86 2) $0.46 3) $9.32
4) $6.87 5) $0.35 6) $2.08

Day 15:
1) One-dollar bill 2) Five-dollar bill
3) Ten-dollar bill
4) $1.00 5) $5.00 6) $10.00
7) $11.00 8) $21.00 9) $32.00 10) $36.00

Day 16:
1) $7.00 2) $25.00 3) $18.00 4) $36.00
5) $77.00 6) $62.00 7) $43.00
8) $51.00 9) $80.00 10) $99.00

Day 17:
1) 1 2) 100 3) 3 4) 10 5) 20
6) 15 7) 500 8) 20 9) 5 10) 4

Day 18:
1) $5.63 2) $11.11 3) $16.55 4) $1.27
5) $16.50 6) $10.43 7) $27.05 8) $2.58

Day 19:
1) $53.55 2) $11.59 3) $38.12 4) $29.50
5) $53.65 6) $16.45 7) $34.79 8) $28.63
9) $34.33 10) $22.74 11) $39.71 12) $27.45

Day 20:
1) $27.36 2) $24.85 3) $28.00
4) $17.99 5) $90.00 6) $27.15

Day 21:
1) Twenty-dollar bill 2) Fifty-dollar bill
3) Hundred-dollar bill
4) $20.00 5) $50.00 6) $100.00
7) $121.00 8) $190.00
9) $360.00 10) $171.00

Day 22:
1) $120.23 2) $51.21 3) $221.00
4) $40.17 5) $77.95 6) $248.05
7) $164.77 8) $397.10

Day 23:
1) 4 2) 10 3) 5 4) 100 5) 10
6) $71.05 7) $100.81 8) $60.45 9) $150.30

Day 24:
1) $84.98 2) $229.95 3) $76.47
4) $178.25 5) $74.50 6) $84.55
7) $410.00 8) $240.54 9) $670.00
10) $80.51 11) $80.75

Day 25:
1) $199.96 2) $249.00 3) $21.00
4) $180.99 5) $30.00 6) 16

Day 26:
1) 0, 1, 1, 4 2) 1, 1, 0, 3 3) 2, 1, 0, 1
4) 3, 2, 0, 2 5) 3, 0, 1, 3 6) 2, 0, 1, 1
7) 0, 2, 0, 4 8) 1, 2, 0, 0 9) 2, 2, 0, 2
10) 1, 0, 1, 3 11) 1, 0, 0, 1 12) 3, 1, 1, 0

Day 27:
1) 2, 0, 2, 2, 0, 0, 3 2) 6, 0, 3, 0, 1, 1, 2
3) 4, 1, 3, 3, 1, 1, 2 4) 3, 1, 4, 2, 2, 0, 0
5) 5, 0, 0, 1, 2, 0, 4 6) 7, 1, 1, 3, 1, 0, 3

Day 28:
1) 1, 0, 4, 2, 2, 0, 2 2) 0, 1, 2, 2, 0, 1, 0
3) 1131113 4) 7, 1, 4, 2, 1, 1, 0
5) 9, 1, 4, 3, 2, 0, 4 6) 1, 4, 1, 3, 1, 1, 0, 2

Day 29:
1) $\frac{2}{3}$ 2) $\frac{1}{2}$ 3) $\frac{4}{7}$ 4) $\frac{2}{4}$ 5) $\frac{4}{5}$ 6) $\frac{5}{8}$
7) $\frac{3}{5}$ 8) $\frac{3}{4}$ 9) $\frac{7}{12}$ 10) $\frac{3}{4}$ 11) $\frac{1}{3}$ 12) $\frac{2}{3}$
13) $\frac{3}{6}$ 14) $\frac{7}{10}$ 15) $\frac{1}{2}$ 16) $\frac{2}{3}$ 17) $\frac{3}{4}$ 18) $\frac{1}{4}$

Day 30:
1) $\frac{5}{6}$ 2) $\frac{1}{4}$ 3) $\frac{2}{3}$ 4) $\frac{1}{2}$ 5) $\frac{5}{8}$ 6) $\frac{2}{4}$
7) $\frac{9}{16}$ 8) $\frac{3}{5}$ 9) $\frac{4}{6}$ 10) $\frac{3}{4}$ 11) $\frac{3}{5}$ 12) $\frac{1}{2}$
13) $\frac{3}{4}$ 14) $\frac{3}{8}$ 15) $\frac{3}{4}$ 16) $\frac{1}{3}$ 17) $\frac{2}{4}$ 18) $\frac{6}{8}$

Day 31:
1) $\frac{3}{5}$ 2) $\frac{2}{3}$ 3) $\frac{3}{8}$ 4) $\frac{5}{6}$ 5) $\frac{2}{10}$ 6) $\frac{2}{3}$
7) 1 8) 3 9) 6 10) 6

Day 32:
1) $\frac{4}{5}$ 2) $\frac{2}{3}$ 3) $\frac{2}{4}$ 4) $\frac{4}{6}$ 5) $\frac{1}{7}$ 6) $\frac{4}{6}$
7) $\frac{4}{8}$ 8) $\frac{6}{10}$ 9) $\frac{1}{4}$

*(Problems 10-18 are example answers.
Multiple ways of shading are possible.)*

Day 33:
1) 5 2) 9 3) 5 4) 8 5) 6 6) 8 7) 15

Day 34:
1) $\frac{2}{4}$ 2) $\frac{4}{7}$ 3) $\frac{1}{5}$ 4) $\frac{3}{7}$

*(Problems 10-18 are example answers.
Multiple ways of shading are possible.)*

Day 35:
1) $\frac{3}{5}$ 2) $\frac{1}{3}$ 3) $\frac{6}{8}$ 4) $\frac{3}{4}$ 5) $\frac{1}{2}$ 6) $\frac{5}{6}$
7) $\frac{2}{3}$ 8) $\frac{7}{12}$ 9) $\frac{7}{10}$ 10) 2 11) 6 12) 3 13) 4

Day 36:
1) 6 2) 6 3) 15 4) 14 5) 9 6) 20 7) 2

Day 37:
1) < 2) = 3) > 4) > 5) < 6) >
7) = 8) < 9) = 10) > 11) < 12) =

Answers

Day 38:
1) 2 2) 3 3) 1 4) 2 5) 3
6) 1 7) 6 8) 1 9) 4 10) 3
11) 3 12) 3 13) 8 14) 2

Day 39:
1) = 2) > 3) < 4) <
5) > 6) = 7) > 8) >
9) < 10) = 11) > 12) <
13) = 14) >

Day 40:

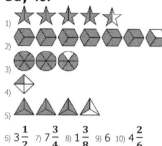

1) 2) 3) 4) 5)

6) $3\frac{1}{2}$ 7) $7\frac{3}{4}$ 8) $1\frac{3}{8}$ 9) 6 10) $4\frac{2}{6}$

Day 41:
1) > 2) < 3) > 4) > 5) >
6) > 7) < 8) > 9) > 10) >
11) < 12) < 13) > 14) =

Day 42:
1) > 2) < 3) < 4) >
5) $\frac{7}{8}$, $1\frac{2}{3}$, $3\frac{1}{2}$, $3\frac{4}{5}$, $4\frac{1}{8}$, $6\frac{1}{3}$, $6\frac{3}{4}$
6) $3\frac{2}{5}$, $3\frac{5}{6}$, 4, $4\frac{1}{2}$, $4\frac{4}{5}$, $5\frac{1}{6}$, $5\frac{1}{3}$

Day 43:
1) $\frac{6}{8}$ 2) $\frac{3}{5}$ 3) $\frac{7}{10}$ 4) $\frac{4}{6}$ 5) $\frac{3}{4}$ 6) $\frac{2}{3}$
7) $\frac{2}{3}$ 8) $\frac{4}{5}$ 9) $\frac{9}{12}$ 10) $\frac{4}{6}$

Day 44:
1) $\frac{3}{6}$ 2) $\frac{4}{4}$ 3) $\frac{13}{16}$ 4) $\frac{5}{8}$ 5) $\frac{7}{9}$ 6) $\frac{4}{5}$ 7) $\frac{5}{6}$
8) $\frac{11}{15}$ 9) $\frac{3}{3}$ 10) $\frac{6}{8}$ 11) $\frac{11}{10}$ 12) $\frac{6}{7}$ 13) $\frac{3}{4}$
14) $\frac{5}{6}$ 15) $\frac{6}{9}$ 16) $\frac{5}{5}$ 17) $\frac{2}{11}$ 18) $\frac{4}{8}$ 19) $\frac{6}{7}$

Day 45:
1) $\frac{2}{5}$ 2) $\frac{1}{4}$ 3) $\frac{4}{8}$ 4) $\frac{1}{3}$ 5) $\frac{3}{10}$ 6) $\frac{2}{6}$
7) $\frac{2}{4}$ 8) $\frac{3}{8}$ 9) $\frac{3}{5}$ 10) $\frac{2}{6}$

Day 46:
1) $\frac{1}{6}$ 2) 0 3) $\frac{7}{16}$ 4) $\frac{3}{8}$ 5) $\frac{3}{6}$ 6) $\frac{4}{9}$ 7) $\frac{1}{5}$
8) $\frac{4}{10}$ 9) $\frac{9}{12}$ 10) $\frac{4}{8}$ 11) $\frac{1}{4}$ 12) $\frac{2}{7}$ 13) $\frac{1}{3}$
14) $\frac{11}{16}$ 15) $\frac{2}{10}$ 16) $\frac{1}{5}$ 17) $\frac{1}{6}$ 18) $\frac{3}{8}$ 19) $\frac{7}{9}$

Day 47:
1) $4\frac{6}{8}$ 2) $4\frac{3}{4}$ 3) $5\frac{3}{3}$ 4) $5\frac{1}{2}$ 5) $2\frac{5}{6}$
6) $4\frac{3}{4}$ 7) $3\frac{1}{2}$

Day 48:
1) $5\frac{1}{6}$ 2) $1\frac{1}{2}$ 3) $3\frac{4}{5}$ 4) 4
5) $8\frac{3}{4}$ 6) $6\frac{5}{6}$ 7) $8\frac{2}{3}$ 8) $5\frac{2}{7}$
9) $11\frac{4}{5}$ 10) $5\frac{10}{16}$ 11) $4\frac{2}{4}$ 12) $6\frac{5}{8}$
13) $12\frac{1}{2}$ 14) $5\frac{5}{7}$ 15) $5\frac{8}{9}$ 16) $6\frac{6}{10}$

Day 49:
1) $3\frac{2}{2}$ 2) $4\frac{8}{6}$ 3) $4\frac{4}{4}$ 4) $6\frac{2}{2}$ 5) $3\frac{4}{3}$
6) $2\frac{9}{6}$ 7) $3\frac{8}{8}$

Day 50:
1) $4\frac{3}{3}$ 2) $2\frac{6}{4}$ 3) $2\frac{6}{5}$ 4) $6\frac{13}{8}$
5) $7\frac{5}{4}$ 6) $6\frac{9}{7}$ 7) $1\frac{3}{5}$ 8) $4\frac{2}{2}$
9) $11\frac{10}{9}$ 10) $10\frac{19}{12}$ 11) $8\frac{7}{5}$ 12) $6\frac{8}{8}$
13) $11\frac{4}{3}$ 14) $12\frac{7}{6}$ 15) $2\frac{2}{2}$ 16) $9\frac{6}{4}$

Day 51:
1) $8\frac{6}{7}$ 2) $11\frac{3}{3}$ 3) $10\frac{2}{2}$ 4) $3\frac{6}{9}$ 5) $9\frac{5}{4}$ 6) $2\frac{6}{5}$
7) $8\frac{9}{8}$ 8) $5\frac{5}{8}$ 9) $16\frac{6}{6}$ 10) $7\frac{6}{7}$ 11) $9\frac{2}{2}$ 12) $7\frac{3}{5}$
13) $13\frac{6}{4}$ 14) $12\frac{7}{7}$ 15) $4\frac{6}{5}$ 16) $8\frac{2}{2}$ 17) $4\frac{3}{3}$ 18) $6\frac{10}{12}$
19) $6\frac{5}{7}$ 20) $9\frac{2}{2}$ 21) $10\frac{3}{3}$ 22) $3\frac{10}{9}$ 23) $8\frac{7}{5}$ 24) $9\frac{3}{4}$
25) $12\frac{10}{8}$ 26) $11\frac{6}{6}$ 27) $8\frac{2}{3}$

Day 52:
1) 1 2) $2\frac{1}{3}$ 3) $3\frac{2}{5}$ 4) $\frac{2}{4}$ 5) $2\frac{3}{8}$
6) 0 7) $1\frac{4}{10}$

Day 53:
1) 1 2) $1\frac{2}{4}$ 3) $2\frac{2}{6}$ 4) $\frac{2}{5}$
5) $3\frac{3}{7}$ 6) $6\frac{2}{4}$ 7) $1\frac{3}{8}$ 8) 4
9) $2\frac{2}{9}$ 10) 4 11) $6\frac{3}{8}$ 12) $2\frac{1}{5}$
13) $2\frac{4}{10}$ 14) 2 15) $2\frac{1}{7}$ 16) $6\frac{2}{6}$

Day 54:
1) $\frac{1}{2}$ 2) $1\frac{1}{2}$ 3) $1\frac{4}{5}$ 4) $1\frac{2}{3}$ 5) 3
6) $\frac{3}{4}$ 7) $\frac{7}{10}$

Day 55:
1) $1\frac{4}{5}$ 2) $\frac{1}{2}$ 3) $1\frac{2}{3}$ 4) $\frac{1}{3}$
5) $1\frac{5}{6}$ 6) $2\frac{3}{4}$ 7) $6\frac{1}{2}$ 8) $2\frac{3}{5}$
9) $\frac{5}{7}$ 10) $4\frac{1}{2}$ 11) $7\frac{2}{3}$ 12) $2\frac{1}{3}$
13) $1\frac{1}{3}$ 14) $4\frac{3}{4}$ 15) $\frac{1}{2}$ 16) $6\frac{3}{5}$

Day 56:
1) $5\frac{4}{5}$ 2) 4 3) $1\frac{5}{7}$ 4) $2\frac{1}{3}$ 5) $6\frac{4}{9}$ 6) $1\frac{5}{8}$
7) $\frac{1}{2}$ 8) $3\frac{1}{3}$ 9) $5\frac{3}{4}$ 10) $3\frac{5}{9}$ 11) $2\frac{2}{7}$ 12) $1\frac{4}{5}$
13) 2 14) $3\frac{1}{2}$ 15) $3\frac{1}{5}$ 16) $\frac{3}{4}$ 17) $4\frac{1}{4}$ 18) $4\frac{1}{3}$
19) $4\frac{2}{3}$ 20) $2\frac{2}{3}$ 21) $4\frac{3}{5}$ 22) 2 23) $8\frac{1}{7}$ 24) $6\frac{3}{7}$
25) $\frac{3}{5}$ 26) 2 27) $1\frac{1}{2}$

Day 57:
1) B 2) D 3) A 4) D
5) 8:00 6) 10:00 7) 3:00 8) 1:00

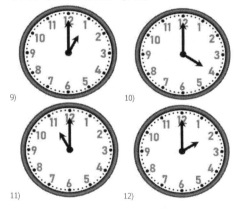

9) 10) 11) 12)

Day 58:
1) C 2) A 3) C 4) C
5) 12:00 6) 5:00 7) 6:00 8) 9:00

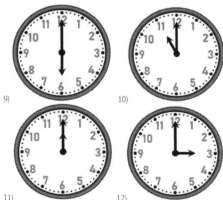

9) 10) 11) 12)

Day 59: 1) D 2) B 3) A 4) B
5) 5:00 6) 12:00 7) 9:00 8) 3:00

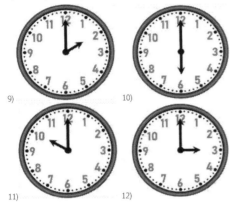

Day 60: 1) C 2) D 3) D 4) B
5) 1:00 6) 7:00 7) 2:00 8) 7:00

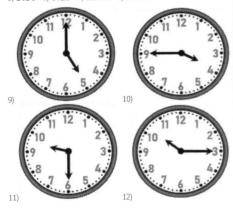

Day 61: 1) D 2) D 3) D 4) A
5) 3:30 6) 8:15 7) 11:45 8) 12:15

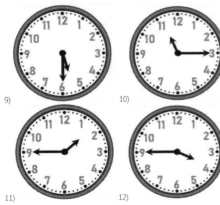

Day 62: 1) C 2) C 3) A 4) B
5) 4:15 6) 9:15 7) 10:00 8) 3:15

Day 63: 1) B 2) B 3) C 4) A
5) 8:45 6) 3:30 7) 6:15 8) 2:45

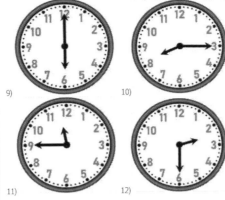

Day 64: 1) C 2) A 3) D 4) D
5) 4:15 6) 12:30 7) 9:30 8) 11:45

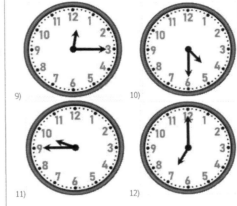

Day 65: 1) D 2) A 3) C 4) A
5) 1:45 6) 9:30 7) 10:00 8) 4:15

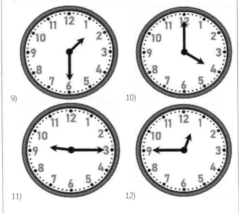

Day 66: 1) C 2) C 3) A 4) B
5) 8:00 6) 4:15 7) 1:45 8) 9:30

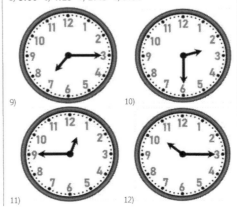

Day 67: 1) A 2) D 3) B 4) A
5) 8:00 6) 4:15 7) 1:45 8) 9:30

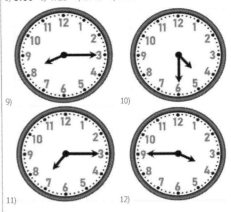

Day 68: 1) A 2) A 3) B 4) A
5) 3:15 6) 12:00 7) 10:00 8) 7:15

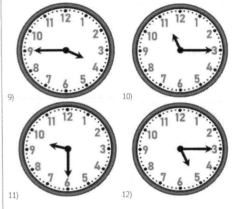

Day 69: 1) A 2) B 3) A 4) B
5) 10:45 6) 7:10 7) 6:50 8) 10:35

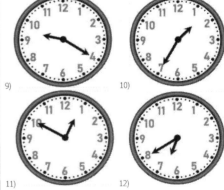

Day 70: 1) C 2) A 3) B 4) D
5) 4:25 6) 2:05 7) 7:55 8) 5:00

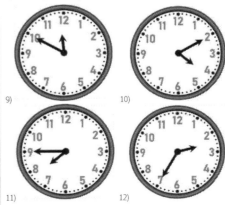

Day 71: 1) D 2) B 3) A 4) C
5) 12:05 6) 10:20 7) 2:30 8) 9:15

Day 75: 1) C 2) B 3) B 4) A
5) 6:15 6) 10:10 7) 11:05 8) 12:05

Day 79: 1) B 2) D 3) C 4) A
5) 9:53 6) 3:54 7) 7:29 8) 4:26

Day 72: 1) B 2) D 3) A 4) C
5) 5:25 6) 5:55 7) 1:30 8) 10:10

Day 76: 1) A 2) B 3) C 4) C
5) 9:25 6) 12:25 7) 6:30 8) 11:30

Day 80: 1) B 2) C 3) D 4) B
5) 1:13 6) 5:14 7) 8:17 8) 3:29

Day 73: 1) C 2) D 3) A 4) C
5) 12:45 6) 7:10 7) 9:40 8) 8:15

Day 77: 1) B 2) D 3) A 4) B
5) 5:43 6) 6:47 7) 7:37 8) 8:33

Day 81: 1) B 2) A 3) B 4) D
5) 8:26 6) 8:11 7) 12:03 8) 11:14

Day 74: 1) A 2) A 3) B 4) D
5) 6:10 6) 3:35 7) 4:20 8) 12:30

Day 78: 1) B 2) B 3) C 4) C
5) 8:09 6) 8:02 7) 5:47 8) 12:47

Day 82: 1) A 2) B 3) B 4) A
5) 1:44 6) 12:51 7) 3:29 8) 3:16

Day 83: 1) B 2) A 3) C 4) A
5) 3:28 6) 4:42 7) 12:59 8) 3:41

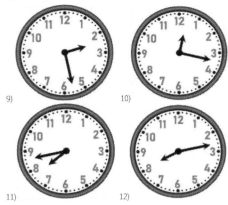

9) 10)
11) 12)

Day 84: 1) B 2) B 3) D 4) A
5) 12:44 6) 1:47 7) 8:59 8) 9:41

9) 10)
11) 12)

Day 85: 1) C 2) A 3) B 4) C
5) 11:09 6) 1:19 7) 11:23 8) 9:32

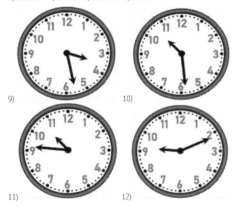

9) 10)
11) 12)

Day 86: 1) A 2) B 3) B 4) C
5) 6:46 6) 12:52 7) 1:57 8) 9:59

9) 10)
11) 12)

Day 87:

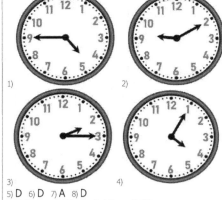

1) 2)
3) 4)
5) D 6) D 7) A 8) D
9) 3:28 10) 1:20 11) 0:44 12) 2:28

Day 88:

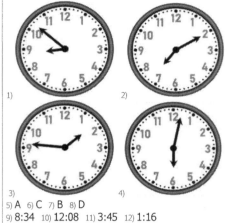

1) 2)
3) 4)
5) A 6) C 7) B 8) D
9) 8:34 10) 12:08 11) 3:45 12) 1:16

Day 89:

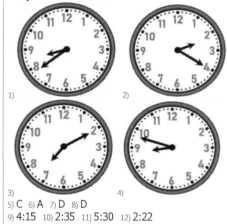

1) 2)
3) 4)
5) C 6) A 7) D 8) D
9) 4:15 10) 2:35 11) 5:30 12) 2:22

Day 90:

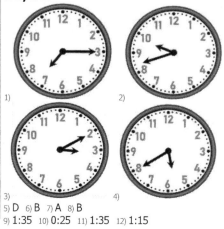

1) 2)
3) 4)
5) D 6) B 7) A 8) B
9) 1:35 10) 0:25 11) 1:35 12) 1:15

Day 91:
1) $25.52 2) $10.81 3) $111.20 4) $71.01
5) 7:19 6) 7:16 7) 12:11 8) 8:03
9) $6\frac{6}{6}$ 10) $5\frac{6}{4}$ 11) $5\frac{6}{7}$

Day 92:
1) $28.25 2) $15.61 3) $30.52 4) $1.86
5) 11:19 6) 2:19 7) 7:26 8) 7:32
9) $3\frac{1}{2}$ 10) $5\frac{3}{5}$ 11) $1\frac{2}{10}$

Day 93:
1) $21.23 2) $101.21 3) $130.60 4) $60.52
5) 6:17 6) 6:23 7) 12:23 8) 5:16
9) $7\frac{5}{4}$ 10) $7\frac{9}{7}$ 11) $2\frac{3}{3}$

Day 94:
1) $120.42 2) $70.80 3) $21.33 4) $40.51
5) 6:54 6) 2:54 7) 11:52 8) 3:08
9) $3\frac{7}{8}$ 10) $2\frac{2}{3}$ 11) $5\frac{1}{12}$

Day 95:
1) $210.00 2) $7.46 3) $30.56 4) $40.21
5) 8:49 6) 3:23 7) 1:21 8) 12:12
9) $7\frac{2}{2}$ 10) $11\frac{6}{5}$ 11) $6\frac{8}{6}$

Day 96:
1) $120.42 2) $101.36 3) $351.20 4) $55.55
5) 5:19 6) 2:08 7) 8:19 8) 6:22
9) $2\frac{1}{4}$ 10) $7\frac{1}{2}$ 11) $2\frac{6}{7}$

Day 97:
1) $5.05 2) $21.66 3) $25.28 4) $100.66
5) 6:26 6) 1:26 7) 12:26 8) 3:26
9) $6\frac{10}{8}$ 10) $7\frac{2}{3}$ 11) $8\frac{13}{9}$

Day 98:
1) $21.38 2) $21.21 3) $21.00 4) $121.95
5) 8:59 6) 12:57 7) 8:46 8) 7:21
9) $\frac{3}{5}$ 10) $3\frac{3}{4}$ 11) $7\frac{5}{10}$

Day 99:
1) $250.00 2) $1.66 3) 71¢ 4) $20.10
5) 5:47 6) 2:52 7) 3:56 8) 5:58
9) $7\frac{6}{5}$ 10) $2\frac{8}{9}$ 11) $9\frac{4}{4}$

Day 100:
1) $60.47 2) $1.81 3) $92.15 4) $200.50
5) 11:08 6) 12:08 7) 6:23 8) 9:32
9) $\frac{5}{7}$ 10) 2 11) $3\frac{2}{3}$

To view more Humble Math books, please visit www.HumbleMath.com.

ISBN: 978-1-63578-325-4

Current contact information for Libro Studio LLC can be found at www.LibroStudioLLC.com

Made in the USA
Coppell, TX
17 August 2020